Naked in the Driveway

Memoirs of a Motherhood Gone Wrong

Laura Fulton

Copyright © 2011 Laura Fulton

Versions of some portions of this collection have been previously published in *Abu Dhabi Week* magazine and are used by permission of Turret Media

All rights reserved

ISBN: 1467911445
ISBN-13: 978-1467911443

For my oldest, my youngest
and the guy with the crinkly eyes

BEFORE THE FOREWORD

If you've seen the trailers for the latest *Mission Impossible* movie, *Ghost Protocol*, there's a great scene in which Tom Cruise scales the outside of a massive golden tower, the Burj Khalifa.

The tallest building in the world (as of this writing), the Burj Khalifa towers over the exotic city of Dubai, a metropolis famous the world over for diamond heists and fabulous wealth. Though it's fallen on tougher times recently, Dubai is still trading on the glamorous image that was portrayed in the second *Sex and the City* flick (which was actually filmed in Morocco - go figure).

The most well-known city in the United Arab Emirates, Dubai is reputedly the playground of Eastern European mob bosses, where banks supposedly hold the funds of major terrorist groups and where millionaire Middle Eastern sheikhs go to have a good time.

About an hour down the road - in a different city entirely - is the sleepy, sensible capital of the country, Abu Dhabi. Unlike it's flashy little sister Dubai, Abu Dhabi is where you'll find lots of families (of every nationality you could imagine), one of the most fabulous mosques in the world and the real wealth of the nation.

In this quiet city, in a villa surrounded by miles of empty desert, one girl from Arkansas is finding that being a mother is a lot harder - but a lot more wonderful - when you actually have kids.

FOREWORD

Appendix A: The Crap Mother Checklist

- Does every drop-off crèche in town know your kids on sight?

- Have you ever asked a bartender to refill your toddler's bottle with 7-Up from the bar gun?

- Do you know how to change your kid's diaper on the floor of a pub restroom?

- Have you ever seen your kid eat an entire piece of birthday cake without using his hands?

- Do you think it's OK to serve your children dinner off a wet wipe instead of a plate?

- Have you ever cooled off all four McDonalds Happy Meal chicken nuggets at the same time by wedging them into the air conditioning vents of your car?

If you said 'no' to any of these questions, then I'm here to make you feel better about yourself because this is just a typical day in my world. If you said 'yes', well, maybe we could all just relax a little. I mean, if the pirates of yore taught us anything, it's that it takes kids a long time to die of scurvy, so yours and mine are probably going to be OK.

That's what I'm hoping for, anyway.

If you've picked up this book, thanks – I really hope that you like it and you like me and you think I'm smart and pretty and funny (but I'd be happy with just funny).

Before we go any further, there are a couple of things you should know:

- This book is based in part on the columns I wrote for a weekly magazine in Abu Dhabi called (creatively enough) *Abu Dhabi Week*. I've tried to group the stories by theme rather than timeline, sp if some details seem out of place, don't worry.

- Though most of these stories happen in Abu Dhabi, it's not really a story about Abu Dhabi. If you want to find out more about what living in the city is like, check out the magazine's website www.AbuDhabiWeek.ae.

- I only have two kids, but throughout this book I say 'oldest' and 'youngest' even though both my mother and my editor have pointed out that grammatically it should be 'older' and 'younger'. I decided the proper way sounded weird.

- Just to nip any potential hate mail in the bud, I'd like to clarify that I always put my children in car seats, they eat enough vegetables that they poop most days and I'm not actually an alcoholic so please don't call Child Protective Services because, however much you may think I deserve it, *no one* will ever love my children as much as I do.

And that just about gets us up to speed.

ACKNOWLEDGEMENT

Abu Dhabi Week is Abu Dhabi's community newspaper. As the name implies, it's both weekly and in English, and it's free – published every Thursday and distributed via pickup bins in the UAE capital's malls, the international airports and a variety of public and private buildings around the city.

Currently *Abu Dhabi Week* has an audited circulation of over 82,000, and just about every single copy is picked up and read. In fact, it's read and reread – the readership survey suggests that the 'pass-on' readership means that each copy is seen by an average of around 2.8 people, which translates into a total readership of nearly 230,000.

The good news is that *Abu Dhabi Week* appears to be both liked and respected by most of the people who open its pages. In the short (but hectic) years since its launch in November 2008, it has become an essential component of the Abu Dhabi landscape, an informative and entertaining read that highlights what's on and what's going on for those who live and/or work in Abu Dhabi.

We've never regarded *Abu Dhabi Week* as a conventional newspaper, though. That role is filled more than adequately by at least four English-language dailies that circulate in the Emirate. Nor do we aim to cover the UAE in the same way that the dailies and other weeklies or monthlies claim to do – in particular, we barely mention Dubai, a hulking presence just up the road which attracts much more than its fair share of attention.

What those other publications can't do is address the needs and interests of the local community in Abu Dhabi. That's what *Abu Dhabi Week* is for – to tell people what's going on, to reflect their interests and concerns, to provide them with a forum and a spokesperson. And the people who write the magazine live and work in Abu Dhabi; it's a magazine for them, too.

For more information, visit www.AbuDhabiWeek.ae

Dennis Jarrett
November 2011

THE GLORY YEARS

I have a police report in my hand that says that the minor fender bender I was in this morning was my fault, but in my defense, I don't think that's entirely accurate.

See, I was in a hurry.

Now, I already wear my hair long enough that I can sweep it back in less than 30 seconds, so getting myself ready in the mornings doesn't take long. Only today, my dear friend Cindy has promised to bring a coffee to me at my office, but I haven't had a pedicure in weeks which means I had to wear closed toed shoes to see her, which means I had to wear pumps, which means I had to wear a dress, which means I had to shave my legs.

Why? Because Cindy can't stand the thought of me with chipped toenail polish and dry skin on my heels. In fact, she would be devastated to discover that there's so much ugliness in this world and would probably slip into the sort of black depression that only gin and Fritos Scoops can cure, and I won't be the one to bring her down.

Despite the extra grooming, I thought I was going to have the kids ready to roll out the door with plenty of time to spare, only my youngest son's teacher thinks he'd be more likely to eat fruit if I cut it up for him, which means I couldn't pack his lunchbox last night but instead had to wait until this morning.

I thought I was very prepared for the day because I had clothes laid out for the kids and had them both dressed and eating breakfast before I went to get myself ready, which was excellent planning on my part until my littlest boy thought he would best serve the interest of leaving on time by impersonating the Incredible Hulk. When I came down to get the kids into the car, I found him not dressed but instead running around the front yard wearing nothing but underpants.

Bad toes and hairy legs and last minute lunchboxes and naked children notwithstanding, I was sure we had enough time to get my oldest son to kindergarten on time. It's become a priority for me ever since I discovered his teacher has been posting his collection of late passes on a sort of Wall of Shame next to the entrance of the classroom all year. No one can say it's my fault he ended up with the most fastidious kindergarten teacher in the whole school.

But we should have been on time.

Only after blazing through town trying to get to the school on time, after getting my son redressed on the front porch (waving good bye to the residents of the other five villas in our compound on their way out) and loading up his backpack full of freshly cut fruit, after whipping back my hair and tending to my legs and turning down my husband for some last minute nookie on the bathroom counter, some idiot had to come tearing across three lanes of traffic and then stop suddenly in front of me. Which means I hit him.

I now have a gaping hole in my front bumper, a traffic report naming me as the culprit, a lunchbox full of brown apple slices and my oldest was perhaps as late as he's ever been.

I nearly invited the policemen to feel my legs and look at my bare feet. I nearly asked them to follow me to my son's school to witness his denigration at the hands of the kinder-Nazi. I nearly asked my baby to demonstrate the speed with which he can get out of his gear and dance in public in his underpants. Instead, I took my police report with poise and grace.

But you can see how it's all only 80 percent my fault. 90 percent max.

* * *

Despite all the bad drivers that run rampant through the streets, Abu Dhabi is a pretty easy place to live, partly because it's way less hectic than a lot of other major metropolitan cities. In fact, at the end of the day, Abu Dhabi is a lot like a small town, one in which it's difficult to keep secrets, so I'm just going to come right out with it. I've been sleeping with a younger man.

A much younger man. In fact, he's only three years old, my youngest son.

He's not nice to have in bed. Last night, I lay awake for hours because the only way he could get comfortable was with his elbow lodged in the back of my neck. They say the love of money is the root of all evil, but I'm inclined to say its sleep deprivation.

There's a reason sleep deprivation has been used as a form of torture the world over for the last several centuries. Lack of sleep can lead to obesity, depression, diabetes and wrinkles. It's been blamed for increased stress levels and poor digestion, so it stands to reason that I should be more strict when my small boys come pattering into my room at two in the morning looking for a cuddle.

They make rotten bed fellows. It's like they grow extra knobby knees and razor sharp elbows in the dark of the night, and they're constantly jabbing my boobs and their father's balls. And while my bed can comfortably accommodate one extra body, the second boy is never far behind the first, which means my queen-sized mattress becomes overpopulated in a hurry.

But every time I'm tempted to take them back to their own perfectly good beds, one of them will invariably roll over, pat my cheek and say, 'I love you Mommy' before curling up against me and falling back to sleep.

Now, I taught high school for many years, so I know that my sweet, small boys will eventually grow into big, sweaty boys who won't want their friends to know I drove them to the mall. Very soon, they'll stop coming in to snuggle and before I know it, 'I love you Mommy' will give way to 'Mom, gross. Stop kissing me.'

So I guess a little sleep deprivation is a small price to pay.

* * *

Now that I've admitted to being the sort of suck mom who can't even enforce a simple 'sleep in your own bed' rule, I'll go ahead and come clean - I let my boys go to bed without a bath last night.

Again.

See, I was at work until 9.00pm and their father only beat me home by a few minutes and the nanny just didn't have the strength to stand up to the boys' protests. They were both having too much fun running around in the yard and enjoying the fresh air to come inside and wash thoroughly. I mean, we live in the Middle East, so for much of the year, it's too hot for them to play outside until after dark.

But let's all take a minute to gain a smidge of perspective.

Neanderthals managed to evolve into the successful species the human race is today without taking a bath every day. Baths for them were most likely accidental if they happened at all - yet here we all stand playing Angry Birds on our smart phones, flying to the moon, discovering alternative fuels, boredom all but a thing of the past.

Alexander the Great managed to build a massive empire without a daily dunk, and Queen Elizabeth the First got on swimmingly despite what must have been powerful body odor. In fact, until relatively recently, baths were considered indulgent at best or dangerous at worst in most parts of the world.

OK, so, all those filthy people before us had to contend with scurvy and scabies and a whole host of other medieval diseases, but they were still able to thrive and create, lead and conquer and none of them let a smidge of grime stand in their way. In fact, most often, they didn't even notice. So if my boys go to bed by the modern definition of 'dirty' two nights in a row, well, they probably aren't going to die in their sleep.

Besides, the oldest has swimming tomorrow, so it would sort of be a waste of time to wash either one of them tonight, don't you think?

* * *

Before I had kids, I never dreamed I would ever put my future children into their pajamas without a wash. But then, I've learned a lot about raising kids since my water first broke. They say that having children makes you stupid, and while I didn't believe it ten years ago, I'm now inclined to agree.

On my way to pick up the kids from school this afternoon, I noticed an odd odor in the car. It took me a while to figure out that the smell was coming from me and even longer to realize that I'd somehow managed to leave the house this morning having put deodorant on only one armpit, losing track of what I was doing mid-torso.

Like *that's* anything new these days.

I sometimes lose my train of thought mid-sentence. I'll wander around my house from one room to another, forgetting where I'm going or what I'm doing or why. I've been known to shave one leg twice and the other not at all, or only get mascara on one eye before drifting away with the fairies.

My children's teachers pity them.

I don't know if I'm biologically less intelligent now or if I'm just constantly distracted and nursing a perpetual case of fatigue. My oldest son is five and a half years old, and if you count the last few months I was pregnant with him, it's been nearly six years since I've been able to go to bed with any certainty that I'll be able to sleep through the night without anyone waking me up.

Whatever it is, I find I'm now just smart enough to recognize how stupid I've become, and it's driving me crazy. Personally, I either want to go back to being as smart as I was before I had kids (and let me tell you, *that* bar isn't set real high) or sink all the way. If I'm going to be stupid, I want to be so stupid that I don't realize I'm stupid - slack jawed and infirm, staggering through my days in blissful...

Has anyone seen my keys? And where on earth did I get this bruise? Was today a free dress day?

Sorry, what was I talking about?

* * *

Discovering that I'm now an idiot hasn't been the biggest surprise of being a mother. I've come to the conclusion that parenting as a profession is the hardest for people who spent any amount of time teaching children in their baby-free days.

As a teacher, you see the very best and the very worst parents – everyone thinks that when they have kids someday, they'll be just like the awesome mothers who turn up to the school in pumps and lipstick with their kids in perfect form. No one thinks they'll be like the ones who look to be hanging on for dear life.

I spent most of my 20s and much of my 30s teaching high school, so you would think that now that I have my own kids, I would have the hang of the whole school thing. I've discovered the hard way, though, that it's a whole different bucket of crayons standing in a mother's flip flops.

When I was teaching, I showed very little mercy to wayward students who strolled into class late. I think I might have even made disparaging comments about the mothers of kids who had no sense of punctuality. For reasons stemming mostly from karma, I think, it seems like the words, 'I would never…' have come back to bite me in the ass with 100 percent consistency. I can clearly remember thinking to myself, 'I would never bring my kids to school late' before I had children.

Now? I understand.

Some days I wake up after lying sleepless all night with one of them coughing to find I forgot to pack their lunchboxes the evening before, and I can find only one Lightning

McQueen Croc and one Bob the Builder Croc but not two that match. On these days, the urgency to get to school on time falls far behind the priority of getting to school at all.

This past week, I was determined not to send my son to school in his uniform on free dress day but I misread the memo and then forgot the proper day. My poor child was the only kid *in the entire school* to arrive out of uniform on a regular day and one of just a few to arrive *in* uniform on the *actual* free dress day.

The good news, though, is that for all my past mistakes, we've managed to get free dress day right the last two times in a row, not because I was able to mark the calendar or send myself an alert on my phone, but because my five year old has started to shoulder the burden of remembering himself.

I'm always impressed that he can remember all the stuff I forget. My own mother was amazingly consistent. She never missed a memo, never dropped the ball on signing forms, never failed to send hand-baked goodies to my teacher for the bake sale.

Unlike me – who thought my mother was omnipresent until just recently – my oldest son has come to realize at the tender age of five that his mom *doesn't* actually know everything after all and that she needs him to remember which days to wear a uniform and which days to wear jeans.

All of which he was going to have to figure out eventually anyway.

We've been late to school so many times this year that I've almost stopped feeling bad about it. The receptionist Lori and I are now on a first name basis, and the classroom assistant knows to wait until 8.30am before recording attendance. I'm sure I'll get it all together eventually. Until then, I'm going to try not to beat myself up about it.

I mean, here's a conversation my son is probably *not* going to have someday forty years from now: 'Senator Fulton, we feel you're the best candidate to lead the free world but our records indicate that when you were in kindergarten, you accrued an excessive number of late passes which may jeopardize your ability to steer our nation through the murky waters ahead.'

If I was a better mother, he'd be crippled by dependency. As it is, he's learning to be independent – and that's *got* to be useful to a future president.

* * *

If my son's going to have any hope of being the president or an astronaut or even a garbage man someday, though, he's going to have to learn how to talk a little better than he does now. No matter how articulate your children are, I think there's always at least some level of language barrier between them and the adult world until they master the art of speaking.

Or maybe that's just my kids.

Take my oldest, who has grossly misinterpreted the definition of 'chicken nuggets'. If you ask him where he got his Happy Meal toy, he'll say, 'It came from chicken nuggets.' They're a food, they're a place, they're a way of life.

This is the same child who once told his kindergarten class that 'my daddy has a lot of money' after my husband pulled ten coins from his pocket one night. His teacher also thought he said, 'My mommy likes to sing on the potty' when he'd actually said, 'My mommy likes to sing at the party.'

The worst misunderstanding, however, happened the day he desperately told me over and over that his brother had 'getted' a lollipop. We were at the bank, and while I was dealing with the teller, the boys performed their usual detailed inspection of every seat in the waiting area, occupied or not.

Now, people across Abu Dhabi give my children candy just for being alive and cute. Clerks keep it on their desks for this very purpose – it's just that kind of town. So when I saw my youngest diligently licking away on a giant red lollipop, my first thought wasn't 'where did he get that?' but rather 'why didn't they give one to his brother, too?'

When I asked where the lolly came from, my oldest son finally explained, 'But *Mommy*, he *getted* it! Nobody *gived* it to him – he only *finded* it on the *seat!*'

It wasn't until then that I realized my smaller son was sucking away on a lollypop someone had started and then left behind.

Perhaps my fair son should start elocution lessons now.

* * *

Or maybe not. Maybe the trick would be to talk to him in broken English and see if he starts speaking properly just so that he can correct me. Logic tells me that patience and consistency are the keys to good parenting, but I've been more and more tempted recently to turn to reverse psychology to get the job done.

I'm coming to that critical junction with my oldest son at which he's starting to think for himself, and most of the time, it's a blessing. He can dress and feed himself, and I've completely forgotten the long months it took for him to make the transition from diapers to toilet. Thinking for himself, however, also means that he can now argue up a storm.

I'm certain that my own mother takes a moment out of every day to relish the thought.

In all fairness, he's a very good boy and I'm lucky to have such a sweet kid, but I've had some interesting arguments with my son. He will insist without wavering that he simply cannot wear the shirt I've picked out for him, he can come up with a hundred reasons why he doesn't need to go to bed just yet and there's nothing I can say to get even the smallest stalk of broccoli into his mouth.

But in some ways, his propensity for arguing is making me a better person.

The other day in traffic, a speeding truck cut me off and I said a word I shouldn't have. From the back seat, my son told me that I shouldn't use that word because 'that's a bad word'. He's insisted I buy the low fat milk with the red cap instead of the full fat milk with the blue cap because 'blue milk makes my belly fat' and that people shouldn't smoke because 'cigarettes are killing'.

Now, I know that when I was a kid, I was the worst for doing the opposite of what my mother said. If my mother told me to stop staring at my sister, I would only stare harder. If she said for me to wash my hands, I might put both palms flat on the floor behind her back just because I could. I have a really bad feeling that all those times I went out of my way to oppose my mother are going to come back to bite me in the butt pretty soon – and hard.

I've now decided, though, that if my son is going to rebel, I might as well make it work for me. I'm considering going out and getting a bunch of skull tattoos. I may buy a motorcycle and start wearing really tiny cut-off shorts, take up a career as a pole dancer and start dabbling in some illegal drugs.

Because if I screw up enough, my hard headed son may turn out to be a great kid out of pure spite.

* * *

Now that my kids have started judging me for it, I've made a real effort to stop using bad words (in front of them), but in my defense, I usually have a pretty good reason.

For everything that's great about living in Abu Dhabi, it's a place where a huge percentage of drivers seem to be in a huge hurry a huge amount of the time. Almost every day, someone comes roaring up behind me driving way over the speed limit. In their panic to get me to move out of their way, they'll ride my back bumper, flashing their lights and honking their horns. It drives me so crazy that I don't always stop myself from screaming at them.

One morning, my sons learned a particularly unsavory word when a quick thinking truck driver saved all of our lives. Traffic had suddenly stopped in front of us thanks to a careless speeding driver in a Mercedes who cut across four lanes of cars trying to make an exit.

The trucker managed to pull into the emergency lane rather than crush me from behind, but now when my son sees someone speeding, he'll point and say, 'Mommy, look! A dickhead!' as if that's the proper English word for 'someone who drives too fast'.

In fact, my two little genetic sponges in the back seat have the uncanny knack for filtering through 53 acceptable words to hone in on the one profane one to try out with their father. When my youngest son was two, he asked my husband to put on a movie for him one early morning.

'We don't have that movie,' my husband explained. My tender toddler's response to his father?

'Flipping idiot.'

Only he didn't say 'flipping'. He said The Word, the really bad F word that you can't say on TV. As much as I don't want my children to start using these words in mixed conversation – or at all, really – there are certain words they've recently started using that I'm way more worried about.

I'd like to know, for instance, who taught my oldest son the concept of boredom. Surrounded with more toys than he knows enough numbers to count, several shelves crammed with books and a mother who's more than happy to show movies on a hot afternoon, he should have no idea what the word means, but in the last month he's started saying, 'I'm bored.'

This has to stop.

Even worse, they've both picked up the expression 'I hate' to apply to everything that displeases them – my favorites are 'I hate sweating', 'I hate this string on my sock', and 'Mommy, you know that mean lady who hit your car with her door? I hate her.'

(I particularly love it when the verb 'hate' is turned into an adjective – my oldest son inaugurated this usage in sentences such as 'cats that bite are hating', a structure that absolves him of the emotion and places the blame firmly on the cat. But I digress.)

However bad the F word is, I think it's just as important for kids to make the distinction between things deserving of their annoyance and things deserving of their hatred –

which in my opinion should be limited to fire ants and people who harm innocents.

But perhaps the very worst words I've heard my kids use – the ones I've nipped most quickly in the bud – are 'stupid' and 'ugly' and 'shut up' and 'you're not my friend anymore' and any others that chip ever so subtly away at the self-esteem of their victims.

Traditional profanity (at least the sort I use) is just a lazy way of expressing an emotion, usually under duress, when I can't think of anything more creative or witty to say. Insults, on the other hand, are meant to hurt another person.

And I'd rather my boys had a dirty mouth than a mean streak.

* * *

Speaking of bad words and dirtiness, some of the worst my kids have heard came out during potty training, which took a really, *really* long time at our house. I can't speak for the mothers of girls, but I'm convinced that when it comes to boys, the real glory years of child rearing begins as soon as they're able to use the toilet all the time.

Other than the sweetness of the newborn which for many parents is lost in a haze of desperate confusion, I personally think that for boys, the years between the end of potty training and the beginning of masturbating are the main reason people want to have kids in the first place.

I mean, when single people imagine what it's like to have kids, they think of riding bikes and hunting for frogs, not tiny underpants full of crap and finding magazines under the bed with titles like *Dixie's Double Ds*.

Honestly, I think at least 80 percent of my job as the mother of boys is teaching them when to get out that bit my son calls his 'bob' and when to keep it put away.

So when my oldest was in the process of giving up diapers, I threw myself into the project. I cajoled, I bribed, I organized games of Sink-the-Ship in which it was his aim to drown a trio of Cheerios swimming in the toilet. More than once, I pulled over to the side of the road so he could water the foliage that I assume the municipality has maintained around town for this very purpose.

In the bank one evening, standing at the counter conducting vital business, I didn't have much attention to spare between the teller and the baby perched on my hip.

This being Abu Dhabi, however, there were no unattended exits, the security guard was keeping a close watch on my kids and no one else in the lobby seemed annoyed by my oldest son – just a toddler – milling around.

I didn't think to take much note of him, in fact, until he disappeared around a corner. When I was finally able to check, I found him in the act of tucking his 'bob' back into him pants.

He'd just had a wee in the potted plant.

It comes as no real surprise, I suppose, that none of the other customers or employees of the bank had had the heart to come to me in time. Seriously, who wants to begin a conversation with a stranger with the words, 'Pardon me, ma'am, but I think your son is about to take a leak in the bougainvillea'?

What could I do but go along with everyone else, pretend I hadn't noticed and make for the door? To this day I haven't had the heart to see if that plant was plastic or real.

All I can say is, those glory years had better be golden.

* * *

Potty training notwithstanding, I'm having a pretty good time with my kids. A lot of people have said it before me, but I never really understood what it meant to love someone until my children were born. You know that first real day of wellness after you've been ill for a long time, when you suddenly remember what it feels like to breathe deeply and feel good and enjoy being alive? Yeah, it's like that.

Still, raising children can be hard work, and even good parents have been tempted to turn to technology for a little help.

While I understand the argument that television is bad for kids, I'm not the only parent I know to contend that the greatest invention of the modern age is the portable DVD player. Seriously, how many young lives have been saved because they were sitting quietly watching a movie rather than driving their parents insane?

Besides, there's a difference between letting kids sit slack jawed in front of endless hours of television and letting them watch a movie that has a finite beginning, a well constructed plot line and distinctive theme music you can hear from the next room to mark the ending.

Even better, many kids' movies these days offer certain educational value. Both of my boys learned how to take off their shirts by themselves after watching the Incredible Hulk in action. Spiderman and the Fantastic Four taught them that sometimes you can turn a horrible science accident to your advantage, and Ironman and Batman both teach that if you're an ingenious billionaire you can be whatever you want in this life, including a super hero.

Of course, these films have now been banned from my house because I know if I put them on, I'll find my kids locked in fierce hand-to-hand super hero combat long before the closing credits start to roll.

I have an even bigger problem when it comes to most of Walt Disney's movies. His flimsy heroines are almost always either helpless or dressed like hookers or both. Disney's step parents are consistently portrayed as evil and our friend Walt has killed off hoards of mothers without a blink of remorse. Yes, I know we live in a world where parents sometimes die, but my kids don't need to hear it from me.

I mean, have you watched *The Lion King* lately? The overriding theme – that whole 'circle of life' thing – is that everybody dies (and sometimes gets eaten), but also that you'd better keep an eye on your uncles and anyone else who's suffered facial disfiguration because they might kill your dad and blame it on you. Talk about embedding trust issues.

Even worse is *Finding Nemo*, a story that begins with a scene of horror so macabre that children haven't seen its equal since the death of Bambi's mom. What psychopath thought it was a good idea for small kids to watch Nemo's mother and all hundred of his brothers and sisters get *eaten* by a pointy toothed reptile? At my house, *Finding Nemo* starts on the first day of school – I nearly included 'skip the opening scene of *Nemo*' in my will.

I'd cast Nemo from our collection entirely, but like many modern films, the benefits outweigh the massacre. I mean, it's Nemo's abduction from the reef that I reference every time I need to say 'and that's why you should always do what Mommy and Daddy tell you'.

See? How could that be bad for kids?

* * *

Considering how much work it takes to get a child from infancy to productive adulthood, it seems a cruel irony that moms get punished for doing our bit for the human race. In exchange for propagating the species, we get stretch marks, saggy bellies and permanent memory loss.

Even worse, now that I'm both married and gainfully employed, I'm finally financially stable enough to go shopping and I've even lost enough weight that I can do it without crying, but wouldn't you know there's nothing in the shops I like anymore? When I was 14 and broke, I loved everything the mall had to offer.

It's bad enough that I have to cruise the glamorous malls of the UAE with my two rambunctious boys in a shopping trolley from the grocery store because the double stroller is just too much hassle. It's bad enough that I have to try on clothes with the door to the change room halfway open most of the time so that I can keep an eye on the same two kids.

But what's really untenable is that when I went shopping last weekend, it was just about impossible to find a simple, pretty blouse that didn't make me look pregnant.

When I finally *did* find exactly what I was looking for, I was heartbroken to discover the store selling a $5 slip of fabric for no less than $50, a price so criminal it offended my Puritan sensibilities to the point that I left the store in disgust.

Now, if I was still 14 years old or no bigger than one thigh bone, I'd be able to find tons of reasonably priced clothes. The fact, though, is that I've accepted that I'm over 40 and that there's no reason for me to even bother walking into stores for teenagers. I don't want to look like a teenager and I wouldn't fool anybody if I tried.

And it's not just me.

'I don't want to look like mutton dressed up as lamb,' said my good friend Cindy one day after a fruitless trip to the mall. 'I just want to look like really pretty mutton. I want to look as good as mutton can look so that when I go out, people will say, 'Hey baby – ewe look amazing'.'

Is that so hard?

MIRACLES

'Shot time!'

I'd been keeping an eye on the clock on the dark paneled wall and as it clicked over to 10.00pm, I returned from the bar with two bottles of water and two Flatliners. It was New Year's Eve and tomorrow would be the first day of 2004.

My favorite tequila-based beverage, a Flatliner consists of half a shot of Peppermint Schnapps layered underneath half a shot of tequila - which floats on top of the heavier liqueur - then complimented with just a smidge of Tabasco sauce which, when poured correctly, forms a flat red line between the Schnapps and the tequila. The result is a minty, spicy mouthful of alcoholic goodness, yummy yet kicky.

'Wait for me!' said Lauren, opening a bottle of water. She chugged her water, set down the empty bottle then reached for her shot. Standing six feet tall with an avalanche of dark corkscrew curls falling down her back, Lauren is fit, fun and brilliantly intelligent. At the moment, she's working as a surgeon. That night, it took all the confidence I had just to stand next to her.

'One, two, three – ahhhhhhhhh!'

Shot Time is an exact science that allows for very little margin of error. Jose Cuervo is a good friend of mine, but he's a jealous friend and he expects you to dance with the one you came with. In other words, if you're going to party with Jose, you'd better *only* party with Jose.

Because otherwise? He will Kick. Your. Ass.

Appendix B: Instructions for Executing Shot Time

- Drink one full bottle of water

- After the initial water break, take one tequila-based shot every half hour on the half hour from the time you arrive until the time you leave (plan accordingly so that you don't have to drive yourself home)

- Hydrate between shots with bottles of water or Diet Coke *and nothing else*

- Dancing in the bar – required. Dancing *on* the bar? Optional but recommended

- NOTE: Execute Shot Time the *right* way and you'll have a great night, just drunk enough to have a good time without slurring, stumbling or nursing a hangover the next day. Get it wrong and you *will* be sorry

Tequila ingested, we opened new bottles of water and settled in with our friends at our favorite table in our favorite pub, Heroes, waiting for the DJ to play a good song.

'You look fab!' I shouted to Lauren over the vigorous voices of some British band I'd never heard of blasting through the speakers. To say Lauren looks great is sort of like saying *the sky is blue* or *I blink often* – goes without saying, really.

'Is Joey coming tonight?' she called back, tucking a long dark curly lock behind her ear.

'Naw – that's one more relationship well and truly *over*,' I replied with a shudder. Though I was single again, the silver lining was that Joey had made me really insecure, constantly telling me how he was still considering getting back together with his ex-girlfriend who was a flight attendant ten years younger than me.

As a result, I stopped eating and lost most of the weight I'd gained in the last 18 months since arriving in Abu Dhabi. So that was something.

'Well, you look great,' said Lauren, reaching over to give my arm a sympathetic squeeze. 'He was clearly beneath you.'

'Yeah, I mean, it's just as well – he wasn't The Guy,' I conceded. 'The sooner I move on, the better.'

In all my many (many) years of being single, I'd developed a theory. The minute any relationship crosses the line between Just Friends and Something More, there are only three possible outcomes – you'll either stay together for the rest of your life, you'll break up or one of you will die (OK, I guess there's only *two* possible outcomes). There's nowhere else for it to go. You can only stay together forever with one person, so the *moment* you realize the guy you're with isn't The Guy, best to cut and run.

And I mean *at that very moment*.

The truth was that I wasn't going to bother wasting the rest of my life with a guy who wasn't exactly what I was after. I mean, it wasn't just myself I had to think about. I knew I wanted to have kids and I had to be sure that the dad I picked out was going to be good enough for them.

Appendix C: Characteristics of The Guy
(My Guy, Anyway)

- Taller than I am, enough that I can wear high heels and rest my head on his shoulder when we slow dance

- Older than my younger sister but younger than my older sister (three years either side of me)

- Kind eyes and a nice smile and handsome in general (I'm planning on looking at him for a long time, OK? I'm not being shallow – that's just forethought)

- Not weird about sex (neither too kinky nor too boring)

- Has earned a college degree

- Literate enough to 'get' references to Shakespeare

- Reasonably athletic – enough to stay healthy and look good naked (again, practical) but not so obsessive that he'll be grossed out if I ever get fat

- Not weirdly too rich or completely broke – willing and able to buy me dinner with the understanding that it's somehow his duty (whether I sleep with him or not)

- Not afraid to say 'I love you' to people he actually loves but also not likely to quit his job, grow dreadlocks, start wearing Buddy Holly glasses and try to earn his living singing love songs of his own composition in the subway of any major city

- Passionate about having gainful employment (did I say that already?)

- Capable of holding his own in a bar fight but morally opposed to hitting me

- Fertile and willing to have exactly two children with me

- Doesn't refer to parenting his own kids as 'babysitting'

- Close enough to my religion that I don't have to worship too far outside the box

- Reasonably clean but not a big pansy about getting dirty

- In good health and not allergic to weird stuff

- Not on drugs or likely to gamble us into a second mortgage

- Likes to travel but not likely to join the Peace Corps

- Faithful, even when I leave the room

- Not related to too many crazy people – besides me

* * *

10.30pm – two more Flatliners, two more bottles of water, another dance and Lauren and I flopped back into our chairs, surveying the crowd that had been growing steadily as the time got closer to midnight.

'This sort of sucks that I'm single *again* for New Year's Eve,' I pouted. 'And the worst part is that I can be as funny and pretty and interesting as I want to be – there's still nothing I can do to *make* The Guy turn up. Like, there's no formula that says if I earn this degree and maintain that weight, the father of my children will suddenly appear. Everyone keeps telling me that it'll happen eventually, but will it? Really? Says who?'

'Seriously, don't worry about it,' Lauren the Beautiful reassured me. 'You've got a lot to offer – there's no point wasting your life on a guy who's not good enough for you.'

I wanted to say that the same was infinitely more true about her (and she was single), but she did have a point. I mean, I was coming up on 34 years old, but looking around the table at my other girlfriends – all of whom (including Lauren) were significantly younger than me – I didn't look haggard or crabbed or obviously decrepit.

Sure, I was single, but I was still child-free, I'd run two marathons in the past two years and I knew pretty much every pose of Bikram yoga. I had a master's degree and a good job, and most of my friends laughed at most of my jokes most of the time – I should have been a catch.

And yet...

'Well, I may have a lot to offer *now*,' I said, leaning back and kicking my feet up on an empty chair beside me, 'but you didn't know me when I was growing up. Seriously, if I'm able to snag the sort of guy I really want, it'll be nothing short of a miracle.'

I wasn't holding my breath. In fact, when I'd taken the job teaching in an international school in Abu Dhabi almost two years before, it was largely because I was pretty sure I was never going to get married or have kids. I'd always wanted to see the world and I figured as long as I was unattached, I might as well get on with it.

'Oh, come on,' Lauren scoffed. 'Look at you now with your long blonde hair and blue eyes! You couldn't have been *that* bad.'

'Want to bet? Let me tell you a little bit about me in 1982...'

* * *

It was early in the academic year when we got the memo to take home saying someone was coming to take our school pictures the following week.

I still feel sorry for the poor guy who was pressed into service to take my sixth grade school pictures. Unlike the modern new professionals, this weary photographer made no effort whatsoever to mask the angst of pre-teen politics by posing random groupings of chummy-looking kids into panoramic class shots.

No, my sixth grade photographer simply told us where to sit, when to smile and where to go afterwards in a bland monotone that made us all aware for the first time that adults sometimes lead miserable lives. While he did manage to persuade each of us to choose a career other than photography, he also saved me from making what would have been the worst photographic mistake of my childhood.

In the days running up to Picture Day, I'd spent hours practicing facial expressions in the privacy of the half bathroom I shared with my sisters at home. After many trials and errors, I landed on just the look I was sure was best. I memorized this face, rehearsing it so that I would remember the feel of it just in case I wasn't able to check my look in a mirror in the last seconds before the photographer snapped the shot.

The next day, I stood eagerly in line with the rest of my classmates. I didn't want to make the expression too early because then the other kids might see it and try to imitate it. I wanted to be unique, completely unlike anyone else in my class or even my whole school.

When I took my turn on the stool, I only needed a nanosecond to reproduce the expression I'd practiced in the mirror for so many hours. I bit my lower lip with my two top teeth and then pushed with my tongue until all of my top teeth were covered by my lower lip *except* those two giant, spectacular incisors. It created a perfect Bugs Bunny style overbite, that solitary brace of teeth protruding from my smile.

Now, our photographer took all the school photos of all the children in the entire district. He should have been impervious to surprise but instead he actually did a double take. His camera hand dropped to his side while his other thumb and forefinger applied pressure to the bridge of his nose in an effort, probably, to reduce the migraine headache I was exacerbating with my bunny-tooth smile.

'Don't,' he sighed with all the long-suffering of a man who has spent too many days hanging on the cross of public school photography. 'Don't make that face.'

My scraggly Arkansas classmates and I were surely a poor substitute for the leggy supermodels he'd imagined himself shooting on sandy foreign beaches when he took up the profession. Thankfully, he hadn't been doing the job long enough to give up and just say 'screw it'.

Although that day was surely coming soon.

Taking the time to actually notice the face I was making, he couldn't tell if I was purposefully giving him a hard time or if I really was just that much of a dork. I, of course, cleared up his confusion.

'But I *practiced* this face,' I protested.

'Yeah, well, it looks stupid.'

If he'd said it any other way, if he'd softened his blow by even one ounce, I wouldn't have believed him. As it was, there was no denying his tone, his words or his own anguished face. The shot he finally took caught my expression of indignation which included a slight smile that ended up, all things considered, not so bad.

Which is why, I'm sure, they paid him the big bucks.

* * *

Just a few months later, I was fully responsible for the Episode of the Mistletoe.

It was the last week of school before Christmas vacation when my best friend Shelly and I discovered mistletoe growing in the tree in her back yard. We were eleven years old and had gigantic imaginations. We would spend whole weeks pretending we went to a swank British boarding school and only saw our parents once a year.

I think it was Shelly who pointed out the cardinal mistletoe kissing rule, but of course I was the one to run with it. I was the one who climbed up in the tree and picked a double fistful of the poisonous stuff, determined to take it to school.

'But if we just *take* it to school,' I reasoned with breathless anticipation, 'the boys might use it to kiss other girls, which wouldn't be fair. We have to make sure they use *our* mistletoe to kiss *us*.'

With the greatest reluctance, Shelly found some thread and in her sweet, non-confrontational way followed my instructions. Within the hour, we had each fashioned a mistletoe wreath. At my insistence, we wore these wreaths *on our heads* like crowns on medieval maidens and spent the afternoon in Shelly's back yard commanding imaginary knights to kiss us.

The next day, Shelly wasn't ready for school on time, so rather than meeting her at our regular spot on the sidewalk between our two houses, I had to walk to our elementary school up the street without her.

Undaunted, I wore my mistletoe wreath *directly on my head* – proudly, even. I was the first to arrive at school, having gone early so that I wouldn't miss any of the boys or their Christmas smooches. What choice did they have, I thought? It was mistletoe. They were powerless against it.

When Shelly arrived at school not long later, I couldn't believe she wasn't wearing her crown. After a half-hearted search through her backpack, she stood up and shrugged.

'Sorry,' she conceded, lying without finesse. 'I guess I lost mine.'

'But you *have* to wear yours,' I whined. 'If I'm the only one wearing one, I'll look like an idiot!'

To her credit, Shelly didn't point out that I already looked like an idiot. She also didn't mention that if I was going to look like an idiot wearing the stupid thing on my own, having both of us look like idiots wasn't going to help. Filled with disappointment, I took off my mistletoe wreath and stuffed it into my backpack before anyone else arrived.

See what I'm talking about?

* * *

Throughout that school year, I got completely involved in my mother's old collection of books about the Bobsey twins. Being such a screw-up myself, I was enamored of these teen heroes. The books were about four American siblings living in the 1950s – two sets of boy/girl twins, a mid-teens pair and an almost-teens pair.

All four polite children had naturally Nordic blonde hair and blue eyes, made perfect grades at school, won at sports and said things like 'yes, ma'am' and 'ever so much', as in 'I'd like to go visit the elderly, ever so much!' Their world was a utopia of poodle skirts and sailing on the lake, of sweater vests and saddle shoes, of tiny waists and hands clasped at one's bosoms.

For fun, the Bobsey twins liked to solve mysteries, the main source of conflict in their gentle narratives. To organize their investigations, they had formed a sleuthing club called the Bob Whites, named after a certain speckled bird native to North America famous for making a call that sounds like they're singing the words 'bob white'.

What connection that particular bird had with mystery-solving, I never figured out, but all four Bobsey twins and their equally idyllic friends thought the name quite clever and appropriate. They liked it ever so much.

Sometime around Spring Break in March of the bunny-tooth/mistletoe-wreath school year, after an afternoon spent reading about the Bobsey twins, it seemed like a great idea. I would form a club and have random adventures. If I could be part of a club, then I'd be cool for sure. It was one of those goal-oriented standards of measure, I reasoned – like being a cheerleader or having a boyfriend – that only required the right amount of forethought and planning to achieve.

That night I set to work and the next morning, as soon as I got to school, I put my plan into motion. I approached the coolest kids in my class and gave them each the hand-copied club manifestos I'd produced the night before.

At the top of each list, I'd written The Bob Whites – if the name was good enough for the Bobsey twins, it was good enough for me – and beneath, I'd written the list of officers. Mary Margaret, the smartest girl in class, was to be president with Becky, the prettiest and most popular girl in the class, a close second as vice president.

Carolina, who had the best handwriting in class and wrote the best stories, would be secretary and Louisa, who always aced her spelling tests, would be treasurer.

'What's this for?' Mary Margaret asked. She wasn't being snotty or cruel – she just couldn't make sense of what I was proposing.

'It's for a club called The Bob Whites.'

'But why am I president? Why aren't *you* president?'

It was a reasonable question. If the club was my idea, I should be president, right? But even in the sixth grade, I knew my limitations. I wasn't nearly capable enough to run a club – if I was president, it would be just a stupid club of one, and I was already the president of *that* club.

'I thought you'd be better,' I said, shrugging my shoulders.

'But what are we supposed to do?' Mary Margaret and the rest of the officers waited with furrowed brows for my response.

'Well, we can solve mysteries and have adventures and, you know, like, stuff,' I explained. *Duh*, I thought to myself, *it's like they've never even read the Bobsey twins.*

'But what are *you* supposed to do?' Carolina asked, clearly as confused as the rest of them.

'Whatever you guys want.' *Are you stupid?* I wondered. *What are you not getting about this plan?*

'So, let me get this straight,' Mary Margaret said. 'You made up a club and made all of us officers just so you could be *in* the club, but you don't know what we're supposed to do?'

With a surge of realization in the pit of my stomach, I understood exactly how hopeless I looked to the other girls - all of whom gracious changed the subject, sparing me any further humiliation. Thus ended the first and last meeting of the Bob Whites. I wished I would suddenly fall down dead on the spot.

Ever so much.

* * *

'OK, OK,' laughed Lauren. 'I'll admit - that's pretty bad. But you were only, what, 12 years old? You're not like that anymore. Look at you now! You're gorgeous!'

'Eye of the beholder, my friend,' I conceded, cocking my head and handing her our next shot. 'Do I really need to remind you of what happened in Fujairah *just last year*?'

'I was hoping you'd forgotten,' Lauren sniggered, not able to stop herself from laughing, as if anyone who was there that day would ever forget.

Fat. Chance.

* * *

It was the first long weekend of my first school year in Abu Dhabi, and a group of angry, single fellow female teachers had organized a group trip to a cheap and cheerful resort on the east coast in Fujairah, another emirate five hours away. By the time everyone arrived, we took up most of the rooms and as the sun began to set, every single person I'd met in the few weeks I'd been in the UAE was on the beach.

Lauren was the last to arrive. When she came striding down to the sand, I was already lounging on a sun bed with the lovely Kirsten, a gorgeous British girl ten years my junior with a voluptuous figure. We were surrounded by the handful of breathless young men who always seemed to be on hand whenever Kirsten slipped into a bikini – which was often.

For all of Kirsten's kitten-esque beauty, Lauren is one stunning girl. Also ten years younger than I am, Lauren is a diehard athlete with the body of a swimsuit model. She has a natural ability to play just about any sport and the moxy to go with it. She played on the Canadian National Women's Rugby team for years. When she joined me and Kirsten on the beach, the boys simply sat with their mouths hanging open, eyes pivoting like they were at a tennis match between my two young girlfriends.

'Want to go down to the water?' Lauren asked me, hands on her hips and unconscious of the dumb-struck guys.

'Sure,' I shrugged, getting up from my own sunbed, distracting the boys from Lauren and Kirsten for not even one single second.

'Let's run.'

The only reason I can be friends with Lauren at all is because she's completely unaware of what a stunner she is. When she suggested running, it was for no reason other than the pure, sheer joy of running. So we took off for the shoreline.

Well, Lauren looked like a scene straight out of *Baywatch* with her long, lean legs striding with purpose, hair streaming out behind her, D cups bouncing in figure eights. The entire resort stopped to watch her run, mouths agape.

In the periphery of all those eyes was me – shorter, fatter, clumsy and sweaty, puffing as hard as I could to keep up with the graceful brunette beside me.

I probably would have escaped everyone's attention altogether except that when the land developers built Fujairah into the tourists' paradise it is today, the first thing they did was landscape the coastline so that it could withstand the inundation of the tide.

About halfway across the beach, the level expanse of sand begins to angle downwards. It's not a severe decline, but if you're running as fast as you can and you're more worried about how much your thigh cellulite is bouncing than you are about where you're going, that little angle can come as quite a shock.

This is the point in the film at which everything starts happening in slow motion and the theme music to the Olympic movie *Chariots of Fire* starts playing.

When I came to the spot where the beach begins to slope, my momentum pitched me forward and I couldn't correct my balance. I flailed, clawing for purchase in the thin air until gravity finally got the best of me and I fell. Spectacularly. Knees, then elbows, then a perfect face plant directly into the sand.

Everyone who had been watching Lauren now shifted their gaze to me in horror. And since I couldn't very well lie there sucking beach for the rest of the weekend, I had to stand up and keep going, brushing sand from my eyebrows, ears and hair, spitting it out of my mouth.

And I wondered why I was still single.

* * *

'Yeah, OK, I'll probably never forget that,' said Lauren, giggling with sympathy.

Still, I wanted to believe. Just a week before, I'd seen *Love Actually* at the movie theater and when I got home, I cried and cried, not because I wasn't in love but because all those sweet stories reminded me that, even in the weirdest circumstances, wonderful moments are everywhere, just waiting to happen.

When I was a kid, I believed my stuffed animals could hear me, and I believed that scary things lived in my closet. I believed in fairies and magic and stories and beauty, and I kept on believing even when I grew up. And so, in spite of it all, I believed that sooner or later I would meet The Guy and have my babies.

Because love, actually, really *is* all around.

* * *

11.20pm and I was ready for a quick reconnoiter. Heroes was heaving by this point, and several in the throng looked to be handsome guys. Leaving Lauren at the table with our friends, I went the long way to the ladies room. Above the dimly-lit crowd, one head stood taller than the rest - not enough to make me suspect a glandular disorder but enough that I took notice.

Like a cheetah circling the herd of wildebeests, I sneaked up on his outer flank.

Over the other voices, I could hear him telling a joke with his buddies, and his accent said that he was from Australia - definitely a mark in his favor. Plus he was funny and personable and didn't look to be staring at every girl in the room with his mouth hanging open, panting. But what did he look like?

Staying upwind of the herd, I sidled around, scooting past him under the pretense of going to the bar. He was laughing and his eyes sort of crinkled up cutely when he smiled. He put his hand over his mouth as if to hide his teeth, though - was he deformed? Did he have some weird facial defect he was unconsciously trying to hide?

No. His hand dropped and I saw that he was definitely good looking. Time to go in for the kill.

'Hey, can you tell me what time it is?' I asked, not looking at the cute one but instead talking to a guy who was friends with the boyfriend of one of my friends (yeah, work *that* out) who was standing right near my prey. The herd froze, looking up from their beers in unison. A few minutes of chit chat, and then I turned to Crinkly Eyes.

'So is that a football t-shirt?' I asked with a smile, pretty sure that it was pretty obvious that I was flirting with him.

'Actually it's my favorite AFL team – I used to play,' he said, blatantly turning from his friends to talk to me. When I asked what AFL was, he explained that it was the Australian Rules Football League. I'd seen just enough AFL to know that it's a sport that combines the running and finesse of soccer with the violence of rugby and is rife with big, lean, tough guys who have interesting facial scars.

As we talked, I maneuvered bit by bit until the rest of the herd pulled away and regrouped, leaving Crinkly Eyes alone and vulnerable.

As the 11.30pm Shot Time came and went (unobserved), I asked him more questions and we chatted easily. I found out that when he was in high school, he had been the captain of the football team *and* the cricket team. In college, he was the captain of his semi-professional AFL team, and twice he was voted Best and Fairest by his semi-pro peers, the highest honor in the league.

When he told me he had a double degree in history and politics, I decided it was time to consult my mental checklist of Characteristics of The Guy. Right away, I found myself ticking off items right and left.

And then, just as I was beginning to suspect that I was punching above my weight, it happened.

Reaching behind him to set down his beer on a nearby table, he didn't look at what he was doing and nearly dropped the bottle. A quick fumble and he had it in his hands again, no harm done, but he blushed at his own clumsiness. Hunching his shoulders and shuffling his feet, he looked down at the floor and stammered a little.

'I can tend the rabbits,' he said, putting on the slow, halting voice of the mentally impaired.

Did he?

Did he *really*?

Did he *really*, *actually* just impersonate Lenny from *Of Mice and Men*? One of my favorite books of all time? Could he possibly know how to charm me this much if he wasn't The Guy?

Just then, the countdown began. As the crowd shouted backwards from ten, he gave me a shrug and a grin as if to say 'there's nothing else for it', and right at the stroke of midnight, he bent to give me a chaste but passionate kiss, full of promise and happiness and days to come.

Who says there's no such thing as fairies?

* * *

OK, so I'll admit it. I'm the girl who once dated a guy who lived for six months in the gym of the school where he taught. The same girl who *twice* missed all the signs that her boyfriend was probably married. The very same girl who, in one calendar year, loaned the down payment of a car to two different boyfriends only to see them *both* dump her shortly after, driving away without repaying a penny.

Still, six months after New Year's Eve, the guy with the crinkly eyes asked *me* to marry *him*. Six months after that, we said 'I do' (to each other) and eight days later, I was pregnant with my first baby.

Tell me that's not a miracle.

WELCOME TO MY WORLD

In an act of genetic fair play, my oldest son was born exactly like me while his younger brother is a lot like their father. It's very likely, then, that the little one will grow up to be deft with numbers and a terrible dancer while the big one will be great at making friends and tragically melodramatic.

So when my oldest son started complaining about his shoes hurting his feet not too long ago, I didn't pay a whole lot of attention.

Now, I've slid all the way to the bottom of the slippery slope of children's footwear, allowing my kids to wear Crocs every day, pretty much everywhere. Though the kids had been wearing the same pairs for almost a year, I figured the soft rubber shoes couldn't really be hurting my son that much, even if they were a little tight.

Over the course of the next week, my oldest let me know over and over again – like a tragic, multi-pierced teen actor in a high school production of *Macbeth* – that his shoes were hurting his feet. In my typical rush, I brushed him off with a promise of new shoes and sent him to school anyway, wearing the hateful Crocs.

When we finally got to the store seven days later, the boys had the Lightning McQueen Crocs they wanted picked out almost before we got through the door. Even with a buy-one-get-one-half-off promotion, the shoes were going to be painfully expensive, but I'd promised and there was no going back.

I only needed the next size up for each boy, so I took off my oldest son's shoe to see what size he was currently wearing, and that's when I discovered why they had been hurting his feet.

The week before, he'd stepped on a tack.

All those times he'd complained, the point of the tack had been piercing his foot while the head lay flat against the sole of shoe where I wouldn't notice it. The shoes still fit and were in reasonably good condition, but out of guilt I bought the new pairs anyway.

Because like me, my son felt a new pair of shoes was just the right compensation for all his pain and suffering.

* * *

I'm still astonished, in fact, by how much my oldest son and I are alike. Recently, I noticed that he's developing a ring of tiny little freckles around his right eye, and I'm still not sure how I feel about it.

At first I was excited because I, too, have a constellation of freckles that form a circle of dots around my right eye. It's not so obvious that anyone has ever called me Spot, but it's certainly distinctive. That my son has the same birth mark I have is just further confirmation that I've passed on a little genetic piece of myself for future posterity.

Which, when I think about it, is sort of scary.

See, I'm just a little bit crazy. Not deeply disturbed, wear-my-clothes-inside-out, lock-and-unlock-the-door-25-times insane, but something is definitely not quite right. My desk drawers are all neatly categorized into separate compartments, and all my papers sit at exact right angles in my office. My colleagues mock me.

The clothes in my closet are arranged in a complicated sequence not only by type of garment but also by color so that the entire arrangement forms a perfect arch of fabric – complete with matching hangers – from smallest to largest in sections that move from light to dark (from right to left, *of course*, if you were wondering).

Because anything else? Would be Just. Wrong.

Don't get me started on my kitchen cabinets.

Unfortunately, the same strand in my DNA that makes me store my long socks alongside – but not mixed willy nilly *with* – my short socks was included in the genetic package I passed along to my oldest son.

When he was only 18 months old, I caught my oldest arranging his toy cars in neat rows, keeping the Matchbox brand separate from the Hot Wheels and of course nowhere near the entire range of charismatic vehicles from the Lightning McQueen movies.

And while we're still working on letter recognition, my son's crazy keeps growing in leaps and bounds.

He loves to take a paper napkin, unfold it completely and then lay out his plate in the *exact middle* of his personal placemat. Last night, he insisted on eating with a blue fork and a blue knife to match his blue plate, and he figured out straight away that the green of our IKEA kids' chairs is a slightly different shade than the green of our IKEA kids' table which 'supposedly' matches.

At the age of five, he already sees the innate wisdom of making the bed, bless his heart, and rushes to take up a corner in the morning, pulling the blankets straight and smoothing them out, his pajamas neatly folded by his own hand at the foot of the bed.

Because leaving your pajamas on your pillow would be Just. Wrong.

I love him for that.

* * *

Woven into my oldest son's genetic fabric right next to the Strand of Straightness is his Ladder of Loudness. In the same way people can locate me across the noisiest bars just by following my voice, I always know where to find my oldest son – in the middle of a cluster of kids, telling a story.

At full volume.

And it's not just talking. My oldest and I are likely to be the ones screaming the loudest on a roller coaster, the ones yelling the most for our favorite team. He can't just laugh at what happened in a funny movie – he has to bray so loudly that I can hear him in my bedroom on the second floor even when he's sitting on the sofa in the lounge room far below me.

So you can imagine what our arguments sound like.

The other day he wanted popcorn for breakfast and when I told him no – see? I'm not always a bad mother – he stomped and yelled and carried on.

'This day is *hating*! You're so *mean*! Breakfast is *so stupid*!' he screamed at me.

Not one to suffer a tantrum before my morning coffee, I gave him a piece of my mind right back – loudly enough to wake the neighbors and send the cats scurrying for cover.

'When have we ever had *popcorn* for *breakfast*?!? *I don't care* if you think I'm mean! *WHY ARE YOU YELLING AT ME???*' I screamed right back at him.

Yeah, I get it. Irony is hating.

* * *

For all the noise, I do try to keep the arguments with my kids to a minimum because I have too many memories of pissing off my own mom. It seems that for much of my adult life – most of the years before I had kids of my own, in fact – I thought I was raised by a mother with a permanent frown. That's how I remembered it, anyway.

As I get older, however, it's come to my attention that my mom was actually a very happy person when I was a kid. She's preserved stacks of photo albums which include shots of her laughing and having fun. The biggest grump in my house when I was growing up, it turns out, was me.

Having been confronted with the facts, I've been determined to be a fun mom. I've spent many days trying to instill in my children an image of their mother as a gal who can have a good time – we go to the park, we play silly games, we listen to the Black Eyed Peas.

Trying to jazz up a trip to the grocery store one afternoon, I thought it would be fun to play Race Car, a game that involves finding an empty stretch of corridor in the massive discount grocery store Carrefour, loading both kids into the shopping trolley, running and then sliding to a stop – good times, no doubt. This particular afternoon, I was way too tired for actual running, so instead I gave the buggy an almighty spin.

Now, if you spent more time paying attention to your high school Physics teacher than I did, you can guess what happened next. The silver lining is that my oldest son was content to walk along beside me, so it was only my youngest son holding tight to the back of the trolley when I gave it a whirl.

Gravity being what it is, the spin was enough to launch my son out of the back of that buggy like a meteorite. He went flying, the trolley beneath him jerked right out of his little grip. At one stage, he was actually airborne.

The good news is that he didn't sustain any injuries that couldn't be cured with a bit of chocolate and a Lightning McQueen band-aid. The bad news, obviously, is that while my kids may think I'm fun, they're also pretty sure I'm not very bright.

Inevitable, I supposed, but sooner than I was expecting.

* * *

All of which goes to show that sometimes you just can't win.

When I was single, everyone asked me – ad nauseam – when I was going to settle down. As soon as I started dating a guy, they asked when we were going to make it official. The minute the ring was on my finger, everyone wanted a wedding date and before I could even take off my gown, the most burning question on everyone's lips was when we were going to have kids.

After locating a man, wrangling him into submission, getting him down the aisle and producing a child, the very next question I got was 'when are you going to have another one?' Now that I've come up with a second child to serve as a companion for the first, my friends and family are shocked to hear that I'm done.

Now, on the one hand, I can see their point – my husband was the fourth in a lineup of five children so if his parents had stopped at just two, he never would have been born. All kinds of worthwhile and productive people have been born to parents who already had a couple of kids, I'm sure. In fact, there are moments when I'm a little sad about the kids we haven't had.

While I believe that I have enough love for a whole heap of kids, what I don't have is the sanity.

I think the 'two hands equals two kids' equation makes a lot of sense. As it is, I can put all their stuff in a backpack and still have enough limbs to hold on to both of them at the same time. My two boys have to be friends with each other because they don't have any other options. If I had a third, two of them could pair up and shun the odd sibling – which I know from experience is satisfying until you're the one on the outs.

No, my husband and I have stacked the deck so that we're evenly matched, and as long as we're bigger and smarter, we have the advantage. Let the kids outnumber us?

Not on your life.

* * *

Though I don't want to skew the balance, I do love holding tiny babies and sometimes I think (for just a few minutes) that having another one would be nice. While a lot of kids grow out of their infant sweetness, my youngest seems to stay adorable.

I can truthfully say, without an ounce of bias, that my youngest son is one of the cutest children you'll ever see. His giant blue eyes and sweet round cheeks have prompted half the population of Abu Dhabi to scoop him up and kiss him.

Even so, I cringe every time I see him smile.

When his four top front teeth started going brown a few months ago, I took alarm. I stepped up our daily tooth brushing schedule and gave him so much milk I began to think it would be more cost effective to buy a cow, but nothing seemed to help.

Our first trip to a dentist my husband recommended was traumatic for everyone involved. I cried while I lay in the dentist's chair, constraining my son with both my arms and both my legs as he struggled on my belly. He screamed so hard he threw up all over himself, the dental assistant and me - twice. The doctor finally gave up on the examination after my valiant son bit him for the third time. Under the doctor's orders, I stopped giving my children juice at night.

Months later, a pediatric dentist confirmed that the discoloration on my son's teeth wasn't due to tooth decay. It was, in fact, an indication that the roots of the teeth are slowly dying as the result of a 'mouth trauma', in this case the dive he'd taken off the kitchen counter a year before.

I didn't know my nimble baby could climb the handles of the kitchen drawers until I heard him hit the floor on a day so long ago I'd practically forgotten all about it. From the other room, I'd heard that sickening thud followed by the shallow wail of a child who's truly injured and not just putting it on for sympathy.

Because his budding teeth had taken the brunt of the blow, there was very little blood and because he's a little tough guy, he stopped crying quickly – in fact, I forgot the incident until the teeth started going bad.

It was reassuring to learn that I'd only been a sort-of bad mother on that one day when I let him fall rather than being a completely bad mother every other day of his life by letting his teeth rot out of his head. Still, his smile now looks nothing short of tragic.

If I'm a really bad mother, it's because I've opted against the pediatric dentist's advice to put my toddler under general aesthetic and pay hundreds of dollars for a root canal on teeth that are only going to fall out in a couple of years anyway. Call me crazy.

Speaking of dental activity, my oldest is desperate for his teeth to fall out. When one of his classmates lost a tooth, my son started yanking on his own, hoping to pry one loose.

His desire for his teeth to come out is mainly down to greed. His youthful avarice was awakened when his school friend brought his solitary speck of enamel to school for Show and Tell in a small silk bag his mother had given him to put under his pillow for the Tooth Fairy. Cash for teeth sounds like a pretty good deal to my little boy.

And small wonder. When my dear friend Cindy's daughter lost a tooth this past weekend, the Tooth Fairy kicked in $25 as a reward. I was dumbfounded. $25? For a baby tooth? It wasn't even her first tooth, it was her third, and the little girl couldn't produce the tooth for the fairy's collection because she'd swallowed it. Which is all the more reason for me to let my little one's teeth erode away of their own accord. When I was a kid, I counted myself lucky to get a quarter.

And I thought the *dentist* was expensive.

* * *

Though I give Cindy a hard time for spoiling her daughter, I kind of get it. When I was a teenager, I had visions of bearing a daughter. It wasn't so much that I wanted a daughter more than a son. I just always thought I would have a girl, in the same way I thought I would always live near my mother and keep my natural hair color.

These days, I have to fly 14 hours to take my boys to see my mother, and I can't remember what my original hair color was. And while I don't wish for my children to be anything other than exactly what they are, I sometimes still wonder if I shouldn't have wished harder for a girl.

When he was three, my oldest once insisted I put curlers in his hair, but I'll never spend hours playing 'beauty shop' with my sons the way I have with my friends' little girls.

The boys already look forward to going out for a coffee, but they're mainly in it for the chocolate muffins.

I can't imagine that gossiping with them will ever be the same when their greatest interests are race cars and super heroes. I'll probably never spend an afternoon at the spa with my sons. I'm more likely to spend my time on the sidelines of a muddy football pitch.

But I don't have to wander too far down memory lane before I start looking on my boys with relief.

Any daughter of mine would surely have turned out to be just like me, and I don't know if I could survive ten years living with a teenage girl as petulant and flighty as I was back then. For all the mud and bugs and mayhem, I think I'll take my sweaty little boys. I can handle fist fights and footprints on the floor a lot more easily than hormones and hatred and tears.

Because if anyone's going to be hysterical in my house? It's going to be me.

* * *

Besides, girls will give you a lot more to worry about than boys will. At least, I used to think so. It seems like just yesterday, my babies were crawling around in onesies, chewing on their fists and gurgling – sweet, faultless newborns. All too soon, however, I find I'm going to be a grandmother.

The good news is that both of my boys have done a great job picking out a wife, a delightful woman who is intelligent, educated, witty and fun. She's someone who doesn't mind tidying up the house, who's a great listener and has a good singing voice.

Each of my boys wants to marry a girl who knows exactly how he likes his food and which clothes and sports are his favorites, who will happily bandage his wounds and buy him new underwear, read to him, make sure his teeth are brushed and his bed is made.

I know my boys have both chosen wisely because the girl both of my sons wants to marry is me.

Of course, I've already graciously accepted both proposals and just in the nick of time. This week, our friend departed Abu Dhabi hugely pregnant on the verge of her third trimester. After spending a day with her, both of my sons announced, with every ounce of sincerity, 'Mommy, I have a baby in my belly!'

They're a little young, I suppose, at the ages of three and five, but they've both invited me to lay my hand on their taut, flat stomachs with a loving, 'Mommy, feel my baby kick.'

As fast as time flies, I guess we still have awhile before we need to get down to the nuts and bolts of reproduction.

* * *

While my kids may be a bit behind when it comes to how babies are made, they're remarkably advanced in other ways and I thank our television. Despite all the warnings from anti-TV activists – OK, 'child psychologists' – there are a lot of positive things to be said about many kids' shows these days. Some help teach numbers, letters and colors, some reinforce pleasant messages about problem solving and many encourage fair play and tolerance.

And they almost all come with a soundtrack of really annoying theme music, the sort that drives even good parents up the frigging wall.

Which is why, in a moment of weakness, I caved. One afternoon driving the many miles from the city back out to the mainland where we live, my oldest asked to hear 'The Driving Song'. A quick scan of the six CDs I have on deck turned up only one song that could arguably be about driving – 'Rolling' by the thrash rap group Limp Biskit.

It was a huge hit among the car seat crowd in the back. We listened to it over and over – ditto 'The Lightning McQueen Song' ('Steve McQueen' by Sheryl Crow), 'The Race Car Song' ('We Will Rock You' by Queen) and all the Cowboy Music (the greatest hits of Johnny Cash).

Now, my children love doing their own rigorous renditions of 'The Wheels on the Bus', 'Twinkle Twinkle' and 'The Itsy Bitsy Spider', but when the Barney and Friends live stage show came through town a few weeks ago, they were at a bit of a disadvantage. My kids couldn't keep up with the words to 'Bob the Builder'. They were too eager to get back to 'Rock Your Body' by the Black Eyed Peas, and they're now asking for anything by Lady Gaga.

I can only hope that if they grow up to be rock stars, they'll be able to afford a really nice nursing home for me someday.

* * *

If they do end up being intellectually superior, it may be at least in part because they've been exposed to so many different cultures at such a young age. There are people from nearly every country in the world living in Abu Dhabi, and my kids have had the benefit of spending time with many of them.

Experiencing so many different cultures, though, may be having a negative effect on the development of their first - and let's face it, likely their *only* - language. Recently, after a rummage in the tool box, my oldest son came running up to me with the tape measure in hand and an interesting question: 'Mommy, what is the size of you?'

He was asking how tall I am, presumably with the aim of measuring me, but as I often do, I found his syntax funny but a little disquieting.

Last year, the same child was a member of a kindergarten class of 14 children from 14 different countries. Of the lot, he was the only one who spoke English as his first language. When the teacher emailed the parents a list of student names, his was the only one my Microsoft spell checker could recognize without underlining it in red.

At this tender age, being able to speak English really well in a class of multilingual children might give my son the upper hand. At least without the language barrier, he should be able to understand everything his teacher is asking him to do.

Whether or not that comprehension will translate into good behavior and better marks, however, is yet to be seen. Even worse, as time goes by, his classmates will have the advantage of learning excellent English from their teachers and friends at school plus at least one other language (often two or more) from family at home.

Unfortunately, while my husband and I are in a prime position to teach our children proper English, neither of us has mastered any other language with enough proficiency to do our kids any good – which is why I feel concerned when I hear my son say things like 'everybody isn't here' and 'he don't likes it' which is the logical opposite of 'he likes it'.

I especially loved the day we were going to the shopping mall and we drove past a huge billboard bearing a giant black-and-white photo of the first president of the UAE.

The week before, seeing the same billboard, we'd had a lengthy conversation about His Highness Sheikh Zayed, how he had been an excellent leader, how he was very good at talking to bad guys and making them be nice, how he had gone to live with God, the same God from our church (even if he did practice a different religion).

Seeing the photo again, my son pointed to the former leader and called out, 'Mommy, look! It's Jake Zayed!'

His younger brother isn't much better. This is the same child who's come up with such corkers as 'the dinner man is bringing our food' and 'Mommy, what old are you?' and 'I can't speak Arabic because my Arabic is broken'.

We're working on it. I guess if they're only going to grow up speaking one language fluently, I got to learn them how to talk it real good.

* * *

Language barrier notwithstanding, they're already masters at keeping me company. Recently, when my husband was out of town, I kept myself occupied in the evenings with a book by one of my favorite authors, Stephen King. As usual, each night after I put the kids to bed, I read until I was too scared to read anymore.

Now, I've spent the last five years trying to get my children to sleep in their own beds. But faced with a dark, empty house and Mr. King's fictional heebie jeebies lurking in the shadows of my room, I had no choice – I crept into the kids' room and moved their floppy, warm bodies into my own bed where they both stayed for the remainder of each night my husband was away.

Really, what was I thinking?

Were they meant to protect me? At the ages of three and five, I doubt they'd do much damage against any supernatural incarnation to spring from the twisted mind of the famed horror writer. As tough as they are in battling each other, they'd really be no match against the forces of evil.

I'd be inclined to use the explanation that I thought the bogey man would be put off by their childish virtue and spare them, but one look at the crayon scribbles on my walls and I don't think even the minions of darkness would believe my children are filled with youthful innocence.

I fear my true logic, though subconscious, was that if Stephen King's undead villains came to get me, perhaps they would be so occupied with eating my children that I might be able to get out the window and safely away. I mean, I *did* give birth to them the old fashioned way; I didn't even have an epidural with the little one.

That's not even counting the combined total of 23 months I spent between the two of them breastfeeding, only to hear both of them say their first word – Daddy.

Personally, I think they owe me *something*.

* * *

If they do owe me anything, though, I'm pretty sure the shockingly bad job I'm doing as their mother will even out the score sooner rather than later. I'm well and truly accustomed, in fact, to being out-mothered by my peers. Most days, I'm the only mom running into the school late in the morning with crumbs on my shirt, snot on my pants and dragging behind me two kids eating their breakfast of dry cereal out of plastic sandwich bags.

My friend Cindy, however, has yet to learn the sting of being the worst mother on the block. Her young daughter has never gone to bed without a bath or worn hand-me-down clothes or known a home void of fresh fruit and bread that was baked this morning.

But when her daughter's school decided to 'go green' for Halloween, Cindy wasn't prepared.

The idea was for the parents and children to work together to make costumes from recycled items. A busy working mother, Cindy was at a bit of a loss but came up with what she thought was a pretty good idea for making a black cat costume.

When she arrived on the designated day, however, she found herself – for the first time in her parenting life – utterly outdone. She walked into her daughter's classroom only to find the six-foot-tall mother who looks like a Brazilian super model had fashioned a shark's head (complete with leering teeth) from recycled cardboard.

Beside this talented artist was the mother who had hand stitched a Little Red Riding Hood cape from old curtains and beside *her* was the mom who'd created a realistic interpretation of Thomas the Tank Engine from a carton that had once held a dishwasher.

There Cindy stood, mouth agape, with a black plastic garbage bag in one hand and a roll of tin foil in the other, neither of which are particularly environmentally friendly or recycled. It didn't matter that her daughter was enormously pleased with her costume. Cindy mainly just felt like a right idiot.

Though it was her first trip down Slack Motherhood Lane, it wasn't the first time she'd ever made an ass out of herself.

This year, Cindy's taken up selling jewelry from her home which means that, much of the time, she goes to her customers rather than having them come to her. One day, she'd planned to meet a potential customer who wanted to look at a bracelet. Trying the make the appointment on time, Cindy got stuck in traffic so bad that it took her 45 minutes to travel the two blocks from her daughter's school to the meeting place at the nearby shopping mall.

The midday traffic was suicidal, so when *one more car* cut her off just as she approached the mall, she lost the last of her patience. Now, Cindy is generally the sort of person who would rather walk on her own lips than say something nasty to someone. On this day, however, she was hot and tired and when she slammed on her brakes, her five year old daughter spilled apple juice all over herself and the back seat.

For once, Cindy was not going to take the abuse lying down.

She followed the errant car into the mall parking lot and purposely parked nearby. When the driver got out, pink BlackBerry in hand, it was obvious the woman was in a hurry, but Cindy was at the end of her rope. She approached the woman, hands on hips.

'I know traffic is bad, but there is no reason for you to be so rude,' Cindy began. 'You should know better than to cut people off like that. That sort of behavior is the reason why...'

The tirade went on for several minutes, Cindy's victim standing agape all the while. Without being obscene or offensive, Cindy made her displeasure perfectly clear.

When the other driver at last tried to speak in her defense, Cindy simply put up a hand and walked away. Content with having said her piece, Cindy rushed inside to meet her potential client outside the Starbucks, prepared to apologize for being a few minutes late.

So it was with the worst sort of stomach-turning horror that she found the woman from the parking lot with the pink BlackBerry standing in the designated meeting spot looking around. A quick missed call made from a hiding spot confirmed that the woman Cindy had just berated outside was the very same woman she was meeting to look at the bracelet.

Choking with shame, Cindy finally approached the woman.

'Hi! Do you want to buy a bracelet?' she asked with a nervous giggle, trying – and failing – to brush off the incident in the parking lot.

It turns out the other woman had been sitting in traffic just as long, unable to merge properly because *no one* would let her in. When she'd seen the smidge of available lane, she'd dived in. She'd been in a rush because she was desperate not to inconvenience Cindy, who by now felt like a real moron for having given her tongue free rein. It was exactly the sort of thing I would do.

Welcome to my world, sister.

JUST BREATHE

Thursday, September 22

5.00am

My waters break. Contrary to popular belief, this is not one neat gush with a finite starting and finishing point. You know that moment when you're in the bathroom at a party at someone's house that you don't know that well and you realize that the toilet has started to overflow and there's nothing you can do about it but sneak towels out of the cupboard to slow things down and hope no one notices the Great Flood seeping out from under the door? Yeah, it's like that.

7.10am (2 hours 10 minutes)

My husband wakes up and I inform him of the water situation. At about the same moment, I have my first (tiny, minor, insignificant) contraction.

Realizing it will be hours before anything exciting happens, I send him to work and get up to tackle the housework before it's time to go to the hospital. I wash my hair, shave my legs, iron 11 shirts and clean the kitchen. I am insane.

11.00am (6 hours)

At the insistence of his boss, my husband comes home from work. I call the midwives at the Corniche Hospital, the maternity hospital where most of Abu Dhabi's babies are born. They fear I'll get an infection due to my broken waters, so my husband takes me to the emergency room where they examine me and admit me.

The doctors determine I've dilated about one and a half centimeters, so we get settled in my room (second floor, Ward B, Room 8A) and start walking laps around the ward. Contractions are pieces of cake.

'Pshaw!' I think foolishly. 'I can do this without drugs, no problem!'

Little do I know.

13.00pm (8 hours)

My contractions have become stronger and more regular, but I'm not quite sure if I'm in 'established' labor or simply 'just fuffing around' labor. I have moments when the contractions are five minutes apart, but then they slack off again. I fear I am fuffing.

19.00pm (14 hours)

Wild children are running up and down the corridor outside my room, giving me every reason to question the wisdom of having gotten pregnant at all, but it's much too late now. My husband goes home in hopes of getting some sleep. I give up on walking – simply standing is now quite painful.

The absence of the waters has combined with the pressure of the baby's head on my cervix and suddenly gravity is a cruel joke. Still, I'm in control and even manage to snooze a bit between contractions. I am woman, hear me grunt.

Midnight (19 hours)

I'm quickly losing control as my contractions get worse, I can find no comfortable position in which to lie and I've started throwing up every time I get out of bed. I miss my husband and wish he was with me.

I am, however, relieved to realize that the baby will most certainly be a Libra now, which has been, of course, a rather pressing concern.

Friday, September 23

1.00am (20 hours)

I'm in so much pain I'm certain I must have dilated at least halfway by now, but the midwives are reluctant to check because every examination they perform increases my chance of getting an infection since I no longer have any protective waters between my baby and the rest of the world. After much whining and making of truculent faces on my part the midwife checks and, lo and behold, I have not dilated *one single centimeter*. The midwife thinks I'm a big cry baby and leaves me to dilate like a real woman.

1.30am (20 hours 30 minutes)

I call my husband crying. I casually toss the word 'drugs' into the conversation, but have not yet committed to giving in. My steady-handed husband, who has been wide awake anyway, talks me through several contractions and I manage to find a position in which I can deal with each spasm. It's not ideal as I'm reclining rather than sitting up, but every other position hurts too much. I accept that I might just be a big cry baby and that I couldn't care less.

5.30am (24 hours 30 minutes)

The midwife hooks me up to the CTG, which is the machine that measures when I'm having contractions and how strong they are. She is wholly unimpressed but somewhat concerned that it's been so long since my waters broke and I've made so little progress. Her facial expression seems to suggest that I'm somehow not putting forth enough effort and if I would just get with the program, I might actually give birth sometime today.

After more whining on my part, she says my husband can come back, even though visiting hours don't actually start until noon. I don't use the F word aloud, although it comes to mind.

6.00am (25 hours)

My husband returns and there is much rejoicing. The CTG machine actually makes a bored, yawning sound as it measures my insignificant little contractions – which are killing me, by the way. I peak at 63 on the CTG, although 63 out of how many, I don't ask.

8.30am (27 hours 30 minutes)

The doctor comes and agrees with the midwife that I should be moved to the delivery ward on the third floor. My labor is officially defined as 'established', which I can only assume means it's working, paying taxes, is married and has two kids.

10.30am (29 hours 30 minutes)

The midwife comes to tell me that, due to two emergencies, I'm going to have to wait to go upstairs to the delivery ward. I'm certain I must be dilating like mad and reassure myself that by the time I get there, I'll surely be mere moments away from delivery. I pride myself on having made it this far without drugs. I will look back on this moment with belly laughs.

13.00pm (32 hours)

I am still in my room, as there is still no space for me in the delivery ward. At the insistence of my large, commanding husband, the midwife checks my progress again. He and I are both certain our baby is going to pop out at any moment. Imagine our surprise when the midwife tells us that, after all my crying, screaming and vomiting, I have not dilated *one single bit* and am holding steady at two centimeters.

I throw in all pretense of strength and start crying nonstop.

I confess to my husband that, at the rate I'm going, I simply cannot withstand the number of hours it's going to take for me to fully dilate. I realize at this moment that if I was a pilgrim or a pioneer woman, either my baby or I or both of us would die in childbirth – which makes me feel very lucky and sort of inferior.

The nurse comes to take me up to the delivery ward in a wheelchair. I cry with abandon the whole way, small children in the corridors staring all the while.

I do not care. At. All.

13.30pm (32 hours 30 minutes)

I'm settled in the delivery ward and immediately ask for an epidural but Tressa, my Irish midwife, dissuades me. She suggests I try to make it through with the Entonox gas and save the epidural as a last resort. She promises that in four and a half more hours, she'll check my progress again and we can decide what we should do then. We agree.

I take a deep drag on the gas and suddenly the world is a much better place. After a few contractions with the gas, I decide to get an Entonox inhaler to keep in my purse, as it is lovely, lovely stuff.

17.00pm (36 hours)

Sadly, the contractions have started outsmarting the Entonox. Another examination reveals that I have now dilated a grand total of *three* centimeters. That's it – *three* measly centimeters.

Four doctors and three midwives all agree that my labor is now officially abnormal, that it's not just me being a big fat cry baby and that continuing to do things the old-fashioned way will put the baby's life in danger.

A sudden onslaught of tears seems the only appropriate response.

Everyone, including Irish Tressa, suggests I take an Oxytocine drip (which will make me dilate) accompanied by an epidural. If that doesn't work, they fear I will need a Caesarean section.

'A C-section?!?' I wail. 'After 36 hours?!? Bullshit!!! You can go and...'

At this point, the F word comes out and Tressa calls for the doctor to put in the epidural. Time is an issue as he leaves for the night in an hour. This is Abu Dhabi, after all, so we can't expect a doctor to be on call for something silly like administering an epidural at all hours of the night.

Thankfully my husband is on hand to sign the consent form that allows me to have an epidural at all. I find it worrying on a number of levels that I need *his* consent for the epidural that will manage *my* pain but I refrain from making judgmental comments. Out loud, anyway.

18.00pm (37 hours)

The epidural doctor, my new best friend, sticks my spine full of needles and secures them with three sheets of clear contact paper that cover my entire back.

Within half an hour, I look ghastly with two needles sticking out of my left hand, three drips, the CTG strapped across my belly and the epidural wedged between my vertebrae.

My left leg goes completely numb, my right leg isn't much better. As my head rolled to the side and my eyes roll back in my head, my husband chooses this moment to take some lovely photos for posterity. I remind myself to thank him later but the pain goes far, far away and everything is OK in my world.

19.30pm (38 hours 30 minutes)

The traitorous Tressa leaves for the night.

'Shift schmift,' I think to myself. For no good reason, I feel betrayed. She is replaced by Lynne, a lovely down-to-earth Australian midwife who will see me through.

22.00pm (41 hours)

The Oxytocine is working. My husband tells me the CTG is now reading contractions at 120. You remember all the crying at 63. I decide that the epidural is the cure-all the world has been looking for. Bad hair days, world hunger, international political summits – all of these things could do with the help of a nice healthy epidural, I think.

The doctors come to tell me that I have finally dilated to nine centimeters, and I haven't felt a single one. I'm still throwing up and I keep falling asleep, but I'm happy. I wonder if this is how heroin addicts feel all the time. I suddenly no longer blame them.

Midnight again   (43 hours)

I have finally, finally, finally fully dilated and it's time to start pushing.

It's an odd sensation. I can't actually feel what I'm doing, but I don't want to let on how numb I am as the doctors are hovering around, eager to give me that Caesarean.

Thankfully, I discover that I can see a reflection of what's going under my hospital gown in a sheet of plexi-glass across the room. Lynne runs interference for me, hoping on my behalf to avoid the Caesarean. Watching in the plexi-glass, I see what my body does every time Lynne says 'excellent' and I manage to reproduce that movement when she tells me to push.

Saturday, September 24

12.30am (43 hours 30 minutes)

The doctors decide that, given all the relevant factors, I have exactly two hours to get this baby out and then they're taking me into surgery for a Caesarean. With my husband holding up my dead left leg and Lynne on my right, we start pushing with a vengeance.

1.30am (44 hours 30 minutes)

It's the bottom of the ninth, bases are loaded, time is of the essence and management wants to put in a new pitcher.

The doctors sweep in, deciding that after all this time, Lynne (who is merely a midwife) just isn't good enough and that *they* need to help me push. Because of protocol, Lynne isn't allowed to tell them to get out of the way. Because he's a man and Western, my husband isn't either.

In my delicate condition, I'm left to insist that the doctors let Lynne finish the job. They leave angry, so that on top of everything else, I also get to worry that I've hurt their feelings, but then I was worried about whether or not the baby would be a Libra, so what do I know?

2.00am (45 hours)

We can see the head, but this baby still isn't coming. A true professional, Lynne realizes that at this point, pushing just isn't going to get the job done, no matter who's assisting. In one last ditch effort to save me from the Caesarean, she gets a junior doctor, a girl who is less sure of herself and hasn't yet decided she knows everything.

The young doctor suggests using a Ventousse suction cup to help get the baby out – she wants to give me an episiotomy as well, but I say no. No point cutting open my nether regions unless it's absolutely necessary.

After much asking, then whining, then crying, she agrees to at least *try* to get the baby out without cutting me and promises only to cut if it becomes absolutely necessary. With the head doctor watching over her shoulder, the junior doctor sucks the Ventousse cup to the baby's head and starts to pull. I push with everything I have.

2.10am (45 hours 10 minutes)

With just the slightest bit of tearing, my firstborn son is sucked/pushed into the world with barely a whimper. He is gorgeous. He has a massive bumpy bruise on the back of his head from the Ventousse cup, but otherwise he's perfect.

I end up with just a few tiny stitches, but overall my bits come through intact. On the way back down to my room on Ward B, my perfect baby has a little feed, latching on like a pro. He is absolutely wonderful and worth every single second of the last two days.

* * *

20 Months Later...

Though I spent most of my third trimester terrified I was about to go into early labor, my second son's delivery ended up being much easier than his older brother's.

I couldn't really blame the little guy for not being sure about when I wanted him to come out. Though I understood the conversations were largely pointless, I spoke at length with my second fetus, explaining how he needed to be born during one of the few weeks surrounding his due date that his daddy wouldn't be on a business trip.

I had a very practical reason – as much as I wanted my husband there to hold my hand, the more important issue was the epidural. In those days, according to the law in Abu Dhabi a woman couldn't have an epidural unless her husband or nearest male relative signed a consent form at the time of delivery.

I find this law – and others like it – to be utter bullshit and it's since been changed, but that June, because my next nearest male relative was in Arkansas, I needed my husband on hand to sign the form.

I also explained to my unborn son that I really wasn't in the mood for a Caesarean section and if he could just sort himself out the proper way, I would buy him a bicycle as soon as he wanted one.

In spite of a couple of scares, I had plenty of time in the end to get ready for Baby Number Two to be born. Weeks in advance, I packed my bag for the hospital, cleaned out the closets, scrubbed the fridge and laid out a birthing outfit that was both stylish and comfortable involving yoga pants and layered tank tops.

I even considered bleaching my grout but decided that was just borderline insanity.

As bad luck would have it, my husband left for a business trip to Germany on May 28, and wouldn't you know I spent the entire afternoon of May 29 timing contractions.

I had tried everything to persuade the baby to be born before his father left – walking stairs, drinking saffron tea, creative visualization – but nothing worked.

So of course the moment my husband boarded the plane, I started having contractions. Thankfully they went away when I lay down, but I knew we were getting close. As soon as my husband got home on May 31, I sat down and had a serious talk with my little kicker.

'OK, mister, you need to hurry up,' I said sternly to my stomach. 'Graduation is June 5, and if you want to meet all those high school seniors who have been bringing you presents and patting you all year, you're going to have to come out soon.'

On Friday, June 1, we took the bull by the horns. We spent most of the day walking up to the mall and walking around the wide, cool corridors. I took one very fortuitous three-hour nap and then it was time for our weekly webcam session with my mother. As soon as I sat down to chat, the contractions got more regular.

'Are you OK?' my husband asked as I grimaced in pain. Holding my breath, I decided I could write a dissertation on what a stupid question that is. I started timing and lo and behold, my contractions were coming every five minutes, the definition of 'established labor'.

After he's brother's lengthy delivery, though, I wasn't falling for it. When my husband asked if he should call in sick for the night shift he was meant to start in a few hours, I told him to cool his jets.

At 9.00pm we began waffling in earnest. The pains weren't that much worse than a multitude of others I'd had over the last few months, but once he got to work, my husband would have a difficult time extricating himself. He decided in the end to go ahead and work for just two hours.

Right about then, the contractions gave a little grunt and dug in their heels.

'Are you OK?' my husband asked again. Poor man. I considered hyper-extending one of his knees and asking him the same question but refrained.

It was the first time I considered the possibility that this might really be it, so I changed into my stylish birthing outfit. Luckily I'd washed my hair and shaved my legs that morning in anticipation of going into labor. I mean, giving birth is no time for one to let oneself go.

As my husband put his hand on the door knob, ready to leave for work, it happened.

Just like what you see in the movies, my waters broke like a tidal wave. This was like being at the bottom of Niagara Falls, a gusher, a great and mighty flood. This was water breaking in Biblical proportions. And it just kept coming. The birthing outfit I'd chosen was ruined. A quick costume change later into my oldest sweatpants and we were on our way to the hospital.

* * *

Now it was time to consider the time.

Back in the days when my second son was born at the Corniche Hospital, there was only one doctor who was able to put in the epidural needles, and this guy worked banker's hours from 8.00am to 6.00pm. If you had a baby during any of the other fourteen hours of the day, you were out of luck and just didn't get an epidural.

Two traffic lights away from the hospital, I realized that Epidural Guy had gone home for the night four hours ago and he wouldn't be back for ten more hours. The way things were feeling in my underpants, I wasn't going to make it till morning.

As soon as we got to the hospital, I was given a quick examination in the emergency room where I learned, to my great surprise, that I had already dilated four centimeters. Last time, I had contractions for 36 hours and dilated only one measly centimeter. This was progress. Maybe I would be OK without an epidural.

We were sent directly to the delivery ward and the water just kept on coming. I couldn't figure out where it was all coming from. My stomach wasn't getting any smaller, but I was beginning to think we should gather up the animals and build an ark. 'Gross' isn't enough to describe it. 'Grisly' is a little closer.

By 10.45pm, I was outfitted in my hospital digs and sucking away on the Entonox gas. At that point, a suspicion began to form and it took a clear shape around 12.20am.

First, my son's birthday was going to be June 2, which is sort of a weird date that I'll never be able to remember, and second, I really wasn't sure if I would be able to give birth without an epidural. I remembered the contractions I'd had with my first baby and these were already worse than those had been.

And I had a long way to go.

The midwife kept showing me a handy wooden board she had with circular holes cut into it to show the size of my cervix at each centimeter along the way. Four centimeters looked huge and ten centimeters looked like the Grand Canyon. I was very afraid.

Shouldn't I deserve a million dollars and a trip to Las Vegas for going it without pain killers, I thought? Don't I at least get a gold star on my file? A t-shirt that says, 'I gave birth without an epidural and lived to tell the story'? Something?!?

The good news was that, after attending the births of four children, my husband finally stopped asking 'are you OK?' with each contraction.

I understand there wasn't a lot he could do or say, but I would think that if I'm in the middle of a contraction and I could fit a lemon through my cervix, I am clearly *not* OK. He finally took a hint from the midwives and switched from 'are you OK' to 'just breathe'.

Around 12.40am, the head midwife, Liz from England, came in to examine me. The contractions now felt like someone was wrenching me open with a crow bar, but Liz only sighed and turned up her nose.

'Hmm,' she frowned. 'These contractions are only moderate and ineffective. I'll be back later.'

Moderate and ineffective? All this pain and you've just given my contractions a C minus??? I tried to imagine what A plus contractions were going to feel like and shuddered.

'Jeez,' yawned my husband around 1.00am. 'I'm so jet lagged.'

In all fairness, he'd been awake a fair few hours by now, having flown in from Germany the morning before, but in my current state, I wasn't able to conjure up even one shred of sympathy. Instead, I suggested he hold my hand through a few of my contractions, thinking a broken metacarpal might do wonders for keeping him awake.

I think the CTG monitor behind my head must have started to climb before I could feel each contraction because, as soon as it started to crank up, everyone in the room got jumpy.

'Take some gas now. No, now,' they all said in unison.

Trying to gain some perspective, I asked how high my last contraction had gone. I was up to 83. I still don't know just how high a contraction can possibly go, but the worst I could remember feeling with my first son before I got the epidural was 63, and after they put in the epidural, the contractions got as high as 126.

And I was only at 83.

'I really don't think I can do this,' I whispered to my husband.

At 2.00am, things took a turn for the worse. I was up to eight centimeters, which was big enough, my athletic husband helpfully pointed out, for me to give birth to a cricket ball. When I needed to pee, I couldn't figure how I was going to make it to the restroom.

'Just go,' shrugged Eldo, the South African midwife.

'What, like, in the bed?' I was horrified.

'Um, trust me, it's fine,' she assured me. I figured that, all things considered, what small amount of pee I might have left in my bladder was nothing. With a naughty giggle, I went and then reached for my notepad.

'2.00am, wet the bed, on way to hell, hand basket uncomfortable.'

Now that I'd made it to the bed-wetting stage, I gave up pretending I was in control and moved directly to feeling sorry for myself. When the next contraction came, I inhaled a deep breath of Entonox gas and screamed it all out.

The midwives took my screaming as an indication that my pains had become significantly worse and scurried in to close the deal. The head gal Liz even assured me I'd have the baby by 2.30am. Ha!

By 2.25am, they twigged that I wasn't in the final stages of labor and was only being melodramatic. Trying to be helpful, my husband took up my notebook and pen and asked what he should write.

I promised my mother I wouldn't tell you what I actually told him he could go do with himself, but it wasn't nice.

At 2.40am, I graduated from bed-wetting to vomiting. Once my stomach was empty, I noticed all the midwives but one had mysteriously disappeared. Apparently, they all thought this would be a good time to go grab a cup of tea. Once and only once, my husband began to suggest I pull myself together and keep my voice down. It was at this point we heard the voice of Beelzebub, the god of the Philistines, growl from my throat.

'I'M IN THE MIDDLE OF GIVING BIRTH! I CAN SCREAM IF I WANT TO!!!!!!!!'

'Sorry, sorry,' he shushed. 'Just breathe.'

OK, really? That's all the damn midwives can think to say, too. I can understand if my husband doesn't know what to say, but these are professional midwives. This is all they do, all day, every day. Give me ten minutes and I can come up with a list of a hundred things to say to a woman in labor that are more constructive than 'are you OK' or 'just breathe'.

'I can't do this,' I sobbed helplessly, no longer possessed of the devil. 'I really can't. How much was that last contraction?'

'100...um, and 16. 116,' my husband lied.

'What?!' The sob turned into a high pitched wail. 'It's going to get worse than this! It's going to get up to 126! And the midwives aren't even here! They don't even care! Make him come! Make him come!'

My husband assured me that the baby was making steady progress, that he *was* coming and that it would all be over soon, but I had already tuned him out. When I said 'make him come', I wasn't talking about my baby.

In my mind, I had decided that there must be some way my talented and persuasive husband could roust Epidural Guy out of his bed and make him come to the hospital in the middle of the night and fix everything.

For the next twenty minutes, I screamed through several more contractions and spent the time in between contractions sobbing that I couldn't do it, that it hurt, that nobody cared and that someone should make him come.

Epidural Guy, that is.

For a few minutes more, I divided my time evenly between sucking on the gas and screaming. Perhaps that was why everyone kept telling me to breathe. As long as I had the gas mask plastered to my face, I was quiet.

And then, mysteriously, I went to my happy place. It was like something out of a science fiction movie. One minute I was in the worst pain I could imagine, like the worst menstrual pain of my life multiplied by a thousand, and the next, it didn't hurt anymore.

It was almost like I was down there in the dark with my new son and I could see where we were going – so I headed for the light.

At 3.20am on June 2, the midwives saw the baby's head and it was time to push. With the epidural, I hadn't been able to feel it before, but I now discovered that I could either push high or push low, and it was the low push that did the job. As I made that last big push, the only clear thought I had was, 'Well, I never have to do *that* again.'

* * *

After giving birth early Saturday morning, my perfect second son and I were released with two clean bills of health on Sunday afternoon. We made it to the high school graduation of my last group of students when my baby was only three days old and we got to see all the seniors before they marched out onto the stage.

So what's it like having two kids? Well, you know that feeling you got when you were learning to ride your bike and you took the training wheels off for the first time and you were riding and your dad let go of the bar on the back and you went whizzing down the sidewalk yelling out, 'I'm doing it! I'm doing it!' and even though you weren't completely sure if you would keep on sailing or crash and burn, you wanted to keep going and going?

Yeah. It's like that.

APPENDIX D:
100 THINGS TO SAY TO A WOMAN IN LABOR OTHER THAN 'JUST BREATHE'

1. You can do this
2. You're stronger than you think you are
3. You're almost certainly not going to die of this
4. I love you
5. You've never been more beautiful than you are right now
6. You're amazing
7. Go sista'!
8. That's the way
9. No, that vein in your forehead is *not* popping out
10. Let's find out if I can fit this rubber glove over my head
11. Remember that time you climbed Mt Kilimanjaro/left your shitty ex-husband/learned to speak Italian? If you can do that, you can do this

12. You're a woman – you're tough
13. Men aren't strong enough to do what you're doing right this minute
14. I'm here for you
15. I know it hurts and I'm sorry
16. You're going to be so happy when this is over
17. Do you want to punch me in the mouth?
18. You know, hospital green is *really* your color
19. That gown is so slimming on you
20. This is all *his* fault
21. Your baby can't wait to see you
22. Hold my hand
23. Look at me
24. Let's do this together
25. Tell me about your baby
26. I've booked you in for a pedicure next week
27. Do you want some drugs?
28. It's OK to scream
29. It's OK to cry
30. Do you want to call your mother/sister/therapist?
31. Focus all your attention on the flame of this candle
32. Listen to the music
33. Grunt louder, woman!
34. You've got this
35. You're doing *such* an amazing job
36. The woman in the next room is a loser compared to you
37. You show those contractions who's the boss
38. Yes, it hurts – don't let the pain own you
39. Thousands of women around the world are doing this exact same thing right now
40. Yes, it *is* a big deal, but you can handle it

41. You actually *do* deserve a medal
42. I'm so impressed with you
43. You're an incredible person
44. Let it go
45. Women do this every day
46. It only *feels* like the end of the world
47. Hang in there
48. It's really only your belly – your butt is still *tiny*
49. You're creating new life right now
50. Tomorrow you get to sleep on your front side again
51. Now aren't you glad you did all that Pilates?
52. So what if you've never done Pilates?
53. Of course I'll still love you, no matter *what* happens to the baby fat
54. Focus on *you* right now
55. Nothing else matters
56. Squeeze my arm
57. I'm so proud of you
58. If you were a cat, you'd have to do this for an entire litter
59. Holy crap! I think I just saw George Clooney/Brad Pitt/Hugh Jackman in the waiting room!
60. What do you think this red button on this big machine does?
61. Show those cry babies in the waiting room how it's done
62. You're not a cry baby
63. The nurse said you were the best mom on the whole ward but she can't tell you that because she's not allowed to show favoritism

64. You're going to do a great job – just like your mother
65. You're not going to turn into your mother
66. You're totally cut out for this
67. Maybe you should go pro
68. You never have to do this again if you don't want
69. I'm turning off the video recorder right now
70. Your doctor is totally hot!
71. The obstetrician said you have the best looking cootchie he's seen in a long time
72. These people are professionals
73. Close your eyes
74. So then Cheryl said, 'Oh, no you *didn't*' and then Sue said, 'Oh, yes I *did*' and that's when they started fist fighting and then…
75. It's margaritas the minute we're out of here
76. Can I get you anything?
77. It's not gross
78. I believe in you
79. Hold on
80. The last contraction lasted ten seconds – let's count through the next one
81. Here we go
82. Yes you can
83. Stay with me
84. Visualize your baby moving through your body
85. This is the most natural thing in the world
86. Frigging Eve – I hope somebody kicked her ass
87. This is the most important thing you've ever done
88. It's OK to say the F word
89. Fill up your lungs all the way and then blow for a count of ten

90. The doctor thinks you've got about [*how long*] to go and then it's over
91. We can burn your maternity underpants now if you want
92. Your baby loves you
93. You're right
94. I appreciate everything you're doing right now
95. Let's see what's on Showtime
96. Thank you for letting me share this experience with you
97. I wouldn't do *nearly* as well as you're doing right now
98. You make this look easy
99. You're almost finished
100. I'll shut up now

OH BABY

The first few days I spent at home after my first son was born were not at all what I had expected. In fact, I've learned through harsh experience that my friend Cindy is right when she says, 'Carbohydrates are the root of all evil' and that expectation is the bane of parenting.

The good thing for me was that my sister had just had her first child about three months before mine was born. Now, my nephew didn't sleep for longer than 45 minutes at any one time for months, and by the time my son was born, my sister was delirious from sleep deprivation. So when my newborn baby curled up on my belly for a nap in the hours after I delivered him, I counted myself blessed and promptly fell asleep after spending an entire weekend in labor.

The bad news was that his composure was partly down to the mild case of jaundice he was born with, thanks to his early delivery. I wasn't worried at all until I took him in for his five-day check up when I learned that, because my milk hadn't come in yet, he hadn't gained enough weight. When the doctors insisted I come back to the hospital to spend a night with my baby under the phototherapy lights, I was terrified.

On my way back home to pack a quick overnight bag, I called my husband.

'Pshaw!' he snorted. 'It's just jaundice – it's no big deal.'

In an effort to comfort me, all my girlfriends told me the same thing. Jaundice isn't serious, they all insisted, and it would probably go away if I just put him in the sun, advice that reduced my stress level exactly none.

Back at the hospital, the nurses strapped a piece of fabric over my son's eyes and laid him in the bassinet under the two giant phototherapy lights. It wasn't long before the glaring lights woke him and with his first wiggle, the protective eye band came off.

Convinced my son would go blind from overexposure to the light, I spent the afternoon patting him and readjusting the fabric to protect his future vision. Around dinner time, I rearranged the lights so that they were positioned over my bed. If I sat up perfectly straight, I could hold my baby in my lap under the lights, feed him when he needed it and keep him cooking. I was just barely able to rest my chin on the cold metal of the light's giant frame.

A call to my mother and it was more of the same – it was no big deal, he would be fine, I didn't need to worry. From his comfortable spot on the sofa in our lounge room across town, my husband kept up the mantra over a six pack of cold beer and a football game on TV.

'If this is no big deal,' I wanted to tell everyone, 'why don't *you* come sit under these gigantic freezing lights? Why don't *you* hold him and nurse him every five minutes? Why don't *you* make sure he doesn't go blind? This is my *baby*! My *first* baby! It's a big deal *to me*!'

Eventually, my son fell asleep. With no TV or even a way to hold a book, all I could do was rest my chin and stare at the wall.

And then my phone rang.

It was my Canadian friend Lance calling from Kuwait. We'd taught at the same school when I first moved to Abu Dhabi and though he'd moved on, like so many of the people I've met since I've been here, we stayed in touch.

He was calling to ask if I thought he should get an aquamarine bowtie and cummerbund to go with the tuxedo he was wearing to a ball that night or should he stick with standard black? We hadn't spoken in awhile and he'd forgotten that it was just about time for me to give birth, but Lance and I are the same type of dork and think the same stuff is funny – if I ever need a laugh, he's a good guy to call.

Instead of moaning about my miserable state, I laughed along as he told me all about his latest adventures in bachelorhood in a country where liquor is illegal. It was the first time I'd genuinely smiled in what seemed like days. I kept up my end of the witty banter and in 20 minutes, all the exhaustion and anxiety of the last week had evaporated.

That laugh – like so many before it and so many since – was just what I needed, just when I needed it. I was myself again, only with a baby.

The next day, they let me take my son home again and at last my milk came in. I'd been told that the surge of hormones that accompany the milk can kick-start postpartum depression but for me, they had the opposite effect. Instead of feeling down, I sat on the sofa in my lounge room, holding my baby and sobbing because he was just so beautiful and I was so, so lucky.

* * *

A word of warning regarding new babies:

Tickling your baby is funny, watching him smile is cute, making him laugh so hard he throws up is neither funny nor cute.

Just so you know.

* * *

As lucky as I felt that day my milk came in, I've had plenty of moments since when I've felt decidedly not so lucky – but they usually pass.

Maybe I just don't remember, but can someone please tell me what the hell I did in my childhood to earn a son who would get up two hours past his bedtime to skulk into my bedroom, ferret out the one permanent marker in the entire house and use it to decorate not only my desk but also my laptop and mouse? I thought I was a pretty good kid, but now I'm beginning to wonder.

My husband says it's karmic payback for all the destruction he left in the wake of his childhood, but I'd like to point out that it wasn't his laptop.

Apparently, my husband was quite the little rapscallion when he was a kid. Of all the kids in his family, he was the only boy, number four in a lineup of five. With three doting older sisters, his baby and toddler years were spent in a flurry of mini-mothers following him around attending his every whim. His mother says he didn't speak until he was way older than two years old – up to that point, he didn't need to talk. He could just point and grunt and his sisters would give him anything he wanted.

When he was maybe five, my husband's family owned a car with a push-button starter. They also had a massive dairy farm in the Australian countryside, not too far from the whimsically named town of Warrnambool. With plenty of room for the kids to roam, his mother was free to focus much of her attention on the farm rather than standing over the kids monitoring their every move.

One day, she was in the kitchen cooking when she heard a strange banging noise. It occurred to her that the noise had been going on for awhile and that each bang was followed by faint giggling.

Further investigation revealed my husband – just a toddler at the time – sitting in the driver's seat of the family car, pushing the start button to make the ancient vehicle lurch forward. With a heave, the car would mount a bed of delicate agapanthus flowers his mother had planted and crash into the side of the corrugated iron garage.

Without a foot on the gas pedal, the engine died as soon as the car bumped the wall. It then rolled backwards down the flower bed where my husband, the rascal, would push the button again, much to the delight of his three older sisters who watched with glee as the dent in the side of the garage got bigger with every bang.

Then there was the car that he remodeled a few years later. Finding an open bucket of undercoat his parents had used in repainting the house, he painted racing stripes down the side of the family station wagon, completing the look with a number seven on each door. His one younger sister – who is now a professional artist – used the same undercoat to paint the lawn mower. His parents got most of the undercoat off the car but missed one hubcap, so for years they drove around with one pink wheel.

My son's love of markers should come as no shock, either. My husband and the same arty younger sister once decorated their mother's freshly wallpapered hallway by gripping black markers in each hand and running up and down the length of the passageway. What they could have been thinking is anyone's guess, but their mother was even less amused by the black stripes along her walls than I was with the drawings on my laptop.

So I shouldn't have been surprised when my oldest son let his artistic streak run wild.

For months, my son would get up and prowl the house after we thought he was long asleep. One night, when we were watching a movie, both of us convinced he was asleep for the night, we thought we heard suspicious noises coming from the kitchen but we were too involved in the movie to pause and investigate.

We eventually discovered my oldest son sitting on the kitchen counter. He'd found four peeled cloves of garlic and had snipped them into tiny pieces with a pair of scissors. By the time I discovered him, he was in the process of coloring himself with the very same permanent marker that I thought I'd hidden out of his reach but with which he seemed to be building a long term relationship.

I could hardly wait to take him to nursery school the next day with permanent marker all up and down his arms *and* all over his face like a five o'clock shadow *and* reeking of garlic.

Even at the time, I could see the humor and I would have taken pictures, but my husband was not quite so amused. The good news was that my Olay skin toner got off most of the marker. Even better, the shaving cream my son smeared all over his face, neck and arms the next morning killed most of the smell.

Once again, disaster was averted.

When I told my mother about the mess my son had made, she sent me this email: *Reading through 1976 diary. We had gone to church one morning in March. You asked your Sunday school class if they had to go to church that night. When they said 'yes', you said, 'Too bad – Wizard of Oz is on.' You didn't get to watch it!*

And here I thought that naughty streak came from my husband.

* * *

Just when I thought having one baby was hard work, along came Number Two. Now, there are certain logistics to consider when you've got one newborn and one toddler younger than two years old, but for me things didn't get really tricky until I spent a few months with no nanny freelance writing after I quit teaching.

For a year, I was at home all day every day with the pair of them ganging up on me – which would have been bliss if I hadn't had deadlines.

One morning, when my youngest was maybe a year old, he had a poop so comprehensive there was nothing for it but to give him a bath. After a thorough washing, I drained the tub, set him on the floor and turned to get a towel.

Finding none on the shelf, I left my little son sitting on the bathmat happily chewing on a toy while I went to the drying rack in the next room in search of a clean towel. As I rushed down the hall, I heard suspicious noises coming from the kitchen.

There, I found my older son sitting on the floor conducting a thorough inventory of the drawer of kitchen gadgets. Thankfully there was nothing too pointy in the collection he'd compiled on the rug, but it was an unholy mountain of clutter and I reckoned the floor probably wasn't overly clean.

In fact, floor cleaning seems to be the weakest in my house work repertoire. I would mop more often but all my floors are tile and they're always streaked when I finish. I can't figure out how my old nanny used to keep it sparkling back when I was still teaching and she was in charge of both my oldest son and the housework.

I've found, however, that if I let the kids walk around after their baths with slightly damp feet, the dirt seems to loosen up just enough that it sticks to their clothes when they roll around on the floor. In effect, I manage to clean the floor at the same time that I do the laundry.

Just good time management skills, if you ask me.

I was just dumping all the kitchen things into the sink for washing later when the phone and the doorbell both rang at the same time. It was my editor on the phone, asking if I could submit my article about fluctuating rental prices in the capital by the end of the week instead of by the end of the month, and the maintenance men were at the door with a ladder asking if they could clean the air conditioning ducts.

While I showed the maintenance men in, I explained to my editor that I was nearly finished with the article and would email it to him the next day. It was just as well I hadn't bothered to mop the floor in the lounge room, I thought, because the maintenance men were notorious for leaving an incredible mess behind and besides, the boys would end up with most of the dirt on their feet anyway when they took a bath...

Oh! I'd forgotten my baby was still waiting for a towel!

When I found him, he was industriously emptying everything from the drawers in my bedside table, unconcerned by his nakedness, and as it turned out, I didn't need a clean towel after all.

He dried of natural causes.

* * *

For all I complained about my son's artistic phase during his toddlerhood, a lot of it was sweet. When I caught him with a pink highlighter in his hand drawing flowers on my pristine white bedspread one day, he told me he was making it pretty for me.

I could call him naughty, but somewhere in those scribbles on my water cooler and decorations on my kitchen window is also a wide swath of independence that will serve him well one day.

But however much that autonomy will help him in later life, it was an absolute pain in my backside when I was trying to potty train him. He was the very last kid in his nursery school class to start using the potty, and for months after I started sending him to school in underpants, he continued to poop in his underpants in the evenings, which is nothing short of an unholy mess.

His younger brother has been in the same phase for longer than I care to calculate. At least he's started sneaking away when he goes, giving me some indication that he's about to unload in a clandestine Ninja move I like to call Crouching Toddler, Hidden Potty.

What he lacks in bowel control, however, my baby makes up for in good looks. In fact, the only thing I can find to criticize about his appearance at all is his ears. Seriously, I've considered sending him to nursery with a hat on because if the wind catches his ears, he'll be airborne. My mother says he'll develop a complex if I don't stop making fun of his ears, but my mother-in-law assures me it's genetic and that he got it from his father.

Besides, if my baby doesn't develop a complex about something, he's going to be insufferable as a young man. He's already handsome, smart, funny, talented and charming. He's just aloof enough to make the little girls pursue him but he gives them just enough attention to make them swoon. He's like the Brad Pitt of toddlers.

And while my little one hasn't quite mastered pooping in the potty, in addition to his cuteness, he's also very smart. Already he knows all the letters of the alphabet, the colors, the numbers – pretty much everything his brother knows – but he won't start proper kindergarten for months.

As glad as I am for his intelligence, though, there are days when I'm up to my elbows in poo and I think I wouldn't mind trading just a smidge of his brain power for some reliable continence.

* * *

Speaking of really smart kids, my sister's son is going to be just like she was. When my sister was a child, she was always the smartest student in her class. She was also very cute and small and had big blue eyes which made her the teacher's favorite nine times out of ten. It also made a lot of her classmates hate her, something I didn't know till she was grown.

So far, her son is showing all the signs that he's going to be just as smart as she was. One night when he was about three years old, my nephew picked up his little Bible from his bedside table. It was story time and he wanted to read it to his parents instead of listening to them read to him. Obviously he wasn't able to actually read, so he made up the gospel as he went along.

Here's how it started and some of the things he 'read':

- 'Something happened and God made all these things and it was so good that he couldn't even believe it. The next chapter is about being good and the next one about being nice to people. When we die, we go to heaven and wait for everyone else to get there. And then we are done and we go.'

- 'And the men were imitation and the women were delightful.'

- 'We should love every single person that comes in our house and be good and be delightful and then we go. And when we go to see God it will be delightful.'

- 'And whoever is reading, the people who are listening should show the person reading the holes in their nose.'

After about half an hour, he said, 'You know, you're really pretty lucky that I'm reading this much – I don't really know how to read all the words in this Bible so I'm pretending and I don't need any help.'

I guess my poor kids are going to have to do the best they can with the genetic hand that's been dealt them. Thank goodness my husband is way smarter than I am.

* * *

When the boys were born, we lived in a high rise building in the middle of the city, but when they were about one and three, we moved into a flat in the suburbs on the mainland. It was in a brand new building so we were the first occupants. All the doors around the flat came with keys and between this thing and that, we never got around to taking all those keys out of the various doors.

One morning, my oldest son thought it would be funny to shut himself and his brother into my bedroom while I was out of the room. Since the key was dangling in the lock right at eye level, well, he couldn't resist turning it and taking the key out of the lock.

When I came back only seconds later, my oldest son was trying to get the key back into the lock but his clumsy little fingers couldn't manage it. My first thought was to call someone like my husband, but we didn't have a land line and my cell phone was in my purse.

Which was locked in my bedroom with the kids.

With no phone at hand, I tried taking the handle off the bedroom door from my side. I don't know what I thought I was going to accomplish, but the only thing I managed was to render the door completely useless. Without a handle, I wasn't able to open the door at all, even if my son had somehow managed to get the key back in the lock and turn it.

Inside my bedroom, my youngest son started to cry. For an instant, I reckoned I could call the fire department. This being Abu Dhabi, though, there are no street addresses. When I stopped to consider how long it was likely to take me to go through the lengthy, painful process of trying to give directions to someone who only barely speaks my language, I abandoned the idea.

Besides, my only phone was locked in the room with the kids, so short of yelling out the window, calling for help was not an option.

My only other thought was to try the patio door. We had a small patio off our bedroom, but I wasn't at all sure if it would open from the outside. We also lived on the middle floor, so if I got out there and the patio door didn't open, the kids would still be locked inside, and I would be locked outside, not able to get down.

By this time, both the kids were starting to get agitated. I could hear them inside, my oldest trying his best to console his brother and not managing very well. Now, I've seen firsthand the amount of damage my two little boys can do to a room - and, more importantly, to each other - in a very short time, so I went for the patio.

I ran upstairs and thankfully my neighbor was home. As far as I could tell, he'd just come home from a grueling night shift because I had obviously woke him. Groggy and not understanding the problem, he let me in. While I climbed over the ledge of his roof top patio in hopes of getting down to the roof of my patio below, I yelled for him to call his boss - who was also my husband.

The helpful thing was that the roof of my patio wasn't really a roof but instead just beams that were spaced widely enough apart that I could slip through. The only really dangerous part was that the nearest foothold was quite far below the roof beams, and that foothold was at the very edge of the patio.

Slowly, I eased myself over the edge of my neighbor's patio roof. If I'd lost my balance, I would fall two floors to the bricks below. Above my head, I could hear my neighbor who, with the mental acuity of an air traffic controller, had come fully awake as soon as I went off his roof. He was explaining the situation to my husband so that in the event that I fell, one of them could get me to a hospital.

With a slide that was faster than I'd intended, my foot found the railing of my patio while I was still able to hold on to the beams over my head. With a wobbly jump, I was on my patio and thankfully, the door opened. In a moment, I'd unlocked the bedroom door and it was all over.

I could feel the bruises on the palms of both of my hands right away, but it wasn't until hours later that I noticed the bruise about the size of a grapefruit on the back side of my right arm, all sustained climbing down through the patio beams. By the next day, it was truly gruesome, but I didn't mind. Of all the possible outcomes, a big bruise on my arm was small potatoes.

* * *

And then there was the time we lost our oldest son.

Now, I've been terrified of losing a kid ever since the very first moment I peed on the stick and it came up with two pink lines. My oldest had given me a proper scare a couple of years before when he wandered off in the giant grocery store Carrefour. For twenty minutes, I ran through the store with my baby strapped to my back, growing more and more panicked. I'd reported him missing to the security guards but none of them could convey the proper sense of urgency I needed from them.

Eventually, they found him. He'd been in the toy department – the first place I looked – only he'd taken the scenic route through the display of giant TVs. Scariest of all was that, at the age of only two, he had come back to me walking serenely hand in hand with a security guard, happy to go anywhere with someone he'd never met.

Two years later, he was four years old and pretty good about staying in his bed at night. He'd stopped getting up to decorate walls with markers and fill the wine glasses with coffee grounds.

By this time we'd moved into a villa with plenty of room for the kids to roam. We knew all the neighbors and were pleased that all the kids in the compound wandered in and out of our house in the afternoons.

One night, I put the kids to bed as usual then sat down to watch a some TV while my husband finished whatever he'd been doing on the computer upstairs. At one point, I thought I heard the front door open and shut, but I assumed it was my husband going out to his car in search of something in his work bag.

Eventually my husband came to join me and we were about to start a movie when a nagging thought prompted me to go check on the kids. While my youngest son was sound asleep in his bed, his older brother's bed was empty. I quickly checked all the rooms, and then checked them again. The third time through the house, I checked all the cabinets and closets.

My oldest son was gone.

Now, my husband has the capacity to be as cool as the proverbial cucumber in stressful situations. Having spent years as an air traffic controller, he can handle some pretty tough moments with aplomb. Those moments, however, are ones for which he's been trained. He doesn't panic because he knows the procedures inside and out.

When I came downstairs, he didn't have a procedure in place to cope when I told him our son wasn't in his bed. We were searching the house one more time when I remembered hearing the front door open.

'Maybe he went outside,' I suggested. A quick look around the compound in the dark uncovered exactly nothing.

'Check with the neighbors!' my husband said, alarm now rising in his voice.

Other than one little girl, the other kids in our little compound of six villas are older than my kids by several years, but all the kids know each other pretty well. It wasn't unreasonable to imagine that my oldest son had decided on a whim to go visiting. What *was* unreasonable was the idea that any of our neighbors would invite him inside to play at 8pm instead of bringing him home.

Still, if there was a chance that he'd gone inside someone else's house, it was worth asking. If I was right, he would be found and if I was wrong, my neighbors would just think I was an idiot.

But they already knew that.

When I rang the doorbell and told Tracy, the mom next door, that my son was missing, she sprang into action. Her husband Daz and her two almost-teen boys Mitchell and Liam dropped whatever it was they'd been doing and rushed to help.

While Daz and Tracy searched the yard, the older boys ran to every other house in the compound checking to see if my son had gone to visit someone else. In a much calmer frame of mind than either my husband or me, Daz and Tracy suggested we check our house again.

By this time, I was well and truly in a prickly-skinned state of panic. I'd run out to the road but he was nowhere in sight. All it would take was one car to run him over or snatch him off the street. With the very worst sorts of visions running through my mind, I ran through my house again, crying and calling for my firstborn son.

He wasn't there.

Thinking my son had perhaps hidden in someone else's house, another neighbor Ian suggested everyone check their own houses. All the closets in all the houses around the compound were searched, but he still didn't turn up.

I was on the verge of calling the police when Tracy suggested the kids check my house one last time. Grace, a little tomboy of a girl about nine years old who lives directly opposite us, was a favorite of my boys. She and her brother Trent along with Mitchell and Liam went through every room of my house.

'If you come out, you can have some ice cream!' the kids called, hoping to lure my son. 'If you come out, you can play on my PlayStation!'

I was in despair. He must have gone outside then out the gate of the compound and onto the street where a car would have picked him up and taken him...

'He's here!' The chorus of the kids' voices was the most welcome sound I'd ever heard.

Thinking of the one thing neither my husband nor I had, Grace and Mitchell had checked behind the open door of the room on the top floor where my son had been hiding. When he heard the panic in my voice, he must have reckoned he was in real trouble and hadn't wanted to come out.

By now, I was so glad to have him found that I couldn't be angry with him, which was perhaps what he'd had in mind by staying quiet when what had probably started as a game ended in his mother crying. Safely in my arms, he started to cry as well, not sure what was wrong but certain it was way more serious than he'd meant for it to be.

All was forgiven and all the neighbors thanked. For a moment, I almost felt like a right git. I mean, seriously, who loses their kid in their own house? In the end, though, I was more overwhelmed with appreciation that my neighbors would leap to help the way they did. What were they going to think? That I'm the worst mother they've ever met?

Yeah, no secret there.

STAND BY...FOR HELL

My husband is really good at a lot of things. He can play golf and cricket better than most, and as an air traffic controller, he can talk to 27 airplanes at the same time while drinking a cup of coffee.

He's especially good at making travel plans. If the internet was a brush, he would be Michelangelo. From cheap rental cars to free upgrades to funky cut-rate holiday homes, my husband generally hits a home run when asked to accommodate the most people for the best price.

Most of the time.

Despite the expense, our yearly family trip to Australia is non-negotiable. Once a year around Christmas time, we assemble – under one roof – his two older boys that live with their mother in Australia and our two little boys who live with us in Abu Dhabi.

In an effort to maintain filial peace, we usually rent a house near my in-laws for our visits rather than pushing the friendship with my husband's family. We'd really rather not find out if my kindly father-in-law might actually be capable of killing us all in our sleep.

When we finally arrived at our rental house one Christmas, I wanted to like it. I really did. It wasn't a bad spot on a half acre lot out in the tiny farming community of Cudgee, just ten minutes down the road from most of my husband's family. Despite the ample space, we were soon none too pleased with the woman who had rented us the house.

To begin with, we hadn't counted on the hefty handbook that came with the place full of regulations and instructions for creating airflow with noisy, useless fans sucking and blowing through open windows without screens. You should know that the flies in the Australian countryside are big and surly – you have to actually flick them from your skin or they'll steal your handbag – so open windows are a big deal.

Through the cracks in the hardwood floors we could see the bare dirt of the ground below. Also, none of the pots and pans were coated in Teflon which meant every sinkful of dishes demanded way more attention than I felt content to give while on holiday.

Still, we were so happy to be there that we were willing to enjoy the place in spite of the crickets in the bathtub and the two mini beer fridges that took the place of one full-sized fridge.

Of course, none of the doors shut properly and we could only refrigerate four beers at a time thanks to the ridiculous little fridges. Strange, considering it was an Australian who first invented refrigeration for the very purpose of cooling beer.

But my patience didn't run out completely until a week into the visit. I'd been so relieved to be on solid ground when I arrived that I was willing to believe our hillbilly slumlord when she told us to ignore the signs that had been posted by the local municipality declaring her tap water untreated and as such undrinkable. She'd been drinking the tap water for twenty years, her handwritten note read, and had never had a problem.

It should have occurred to me then that native born Indians don't get Delhi Belly, but I was inclined to take her word for it. Until, that is, my eighteen month old son picked up a stomach bug so vile that he produced liquid farts every hour for a week and ended up with a horrific, bubonic diaper rash complete with open, bleeding sores.

Also, our family should have spent our last day together finishing the massive robotic Lego dragon my husband had bought for his second son's birthday. Instead we spent the day washing every scrap of linen in the house and battling head lice on all four boys. I can't say my dream holiday should involve my first experience with a nit comb.

In truth, the head lice probably wasn't the landlady's fault. What. Ever. I blame her anyway.

Even worse, only hours before bedtime on our last night, the oldest boy accidently kneed himself in the face playing on a giant bouncy pillow at the park with his brothers. After five hours in the emergency room, he came out with several stitches in his face. Again, for no good reason, I blamed the landlady.

Between the dirt, the flies, the poop, the sores, the stitches, the head lice and the tiny stupid refrigerators, I didn't feel a single ounce of guilt when one of the boys sneezed directly into the silverware drawer not five minutes before we left for good.

For half a millisecond, I considered taking out all of the cutlery and washing it. Instead, I quietly closed the drawer and went to pack, muttering a hearty 'good riddance' under my breath.

* * *

Of course, there was nothing about the house in Cudgee that could come close to the journey it took for us to get there. In addition to the money we'd saved on accommodation, my husband thought we could save a bundle by flying standby.

When the powers that be at Etihad Airways announced that all of Abu Dhabi's air traffic controllers could fly standby in any leftover seats on any of their flights at a significant discount, my husband jumped at the chance. At one tenth the price of full fare tickets for all four of us, flying standby was a great idea.

Like the Titanic.

After packing up, feeding the cat and leaving instructions for our house sitter, we took off for the airport, my two little boys both agog with excitement. Imagine their disappointment when their daddy returned from the ticket counter with the news that eleven passengers who'd paid full price were in line to fly standby ahead of us. We would have to go home and try for the next flight 12 hours later.

After placating the kids for a day, we returned to the airport that evening only to find it was just as full as the morning flight had been. Little wonder - Christmas falls right in the middle of Australia's summer, so it's the time when the most number of people are trying to get there.

In short, we were screwed.

After another night and a hard won battle to convince my three year old that we really would go on the plane to see his two older brothers if he would just go to sleep, we returned to the airport the next day for our third try. One grim look from the ticket agent and we decided to change our strategy and take a different flight into Brisbane that included a layover in Singapore then a domestic flight down to Melbourne.

As soon as we arrived in Singapore, however, things took a turn for the worse. Standing at the end of the causeway was a gate agent with our names listed on a placard. As standby passengers, we were being off loaded. The next leg of the flight was full and we would just have to wait for another flight.

It was at this point that my husband got on the phone. Through hard work and tenacity, my husband had worked his way up from dogsbody air traffic controller to Manager of Air Traffic Control Operations for the entire UAE. There are a few benefits to working 18-hour days and climbing the aviation industry corporate ladder, and one is that you may find yourself with the personal mobile phone number of the vice president of operations of the national airline in your BlackBerry.

Time was a-wasting and there was nothing for it but to pull out all the stops and ask for help where he could. In this case, we decided it was best to start at the top.

The good news was that the vice president was able to pull a few strings and get my husband on the next flight. The bad news was that he could only get on as crew, which meant he would have to fly the entire distance in one of the tiny jump seats the flight attendants sit in for take offs, landings and turbulence. Even worse, the kids and I didn't qualify to fly as crew.

We were stranded in Singapore.

* * *

By this time, it was midnight and my husband's flight was boarding. Taking our one credit card with him and thrusting a wad of cash into my hand, he took off at a run, promising he would book flights for us as soon as he got to Brisbane.

At such a late hour, every single hotel within easy access of the airport was full for the night. I was stranded in a strange city with two kids, just enough money, no place to stay and no way of knowing when I'd be able to leave.

The only reason I didn't burst into tears was Shamani, a gem of a woman who works for the Singapore airport. I don't know if the halo comes with the uniform or if she was going above and beyond the call of duty, but she was able to make a dozen phone calls and score me the very last room at the Crowne Plaza, the hotel attached to the airport. I decided to play it safe and stay put at the airport.

Once she'd confirmed the booking, Shamani helped me manage the kids, who were going slowly berserk with sleep deprivation and hunger, through passport control and to the luggage carousel.

There I discovered that, while Etihad had off-loaded my suitcase, they'd failed to retrieve the stroller. It was mere good luck that the boys thought it great fun sitting on the suitcase while I pushed it on a luggage trolley through the airport, onto the tram and to the hotel. To her credit, the lovely Shamani accompanied us the entire way.

Though I found out later that I could have paid $60 to rent a sleeping 'station' for six hours at the passenger lounge, I was thoroughly pleased with our room at the Crowne Plaza. The hot bath, the room service and the fat, plush bathrobe dried up my impending tears, and a few hours of sleep in the very excellent beds put all of us to rights again.

I had no idea at the time how much I was going to appreciate having had that one good night of sleep.

* * *

While the kids and I were snuggled between 800 thread count sheets, somewhere over southwest Asia my poor husband was sitting upright, facing a cabin of 80 people.

With no arm rests, no tray table, no TV and a butt-level view of every single person who wanted to use the bathroom situated just behind his head, my husband spent the seven hours from Singapore to Brisbane in a state of misery.

At six feet four inches, he's developed a slump in his shoulders because he's perpetually worried that people are looking at him. I can't convince him it's because he's good looking. Sitting for seven hours in a position that makes him look like a presidential candidate about to stand up and make a speech is, for my husband, two doors down from hell.

Even worse, when the flight attendants came by with the cart of drinks, they refused his request for red wine. He was flying as crew, they reminded him, which meant he wasn't allowed to drink alcohol.

Though he doesn't see it, my husband has the mysterious ability to captivate flight attendants. Once on a long flight, he found himself walking the aisles trying to bounce our youngest son to sleep, and one of the flight attendants coquettishly invited my husband to lie down with our son in first class. In fact, these young, pretty women are usually falling over their feet to do his bidding.

So when he asked for wine, he was dumbfounded to hear them tell him 'no'. With a sigh, he suffered in sleepless silence for the remainder of his journey.

Once in Brisbane, he set up shop at an internet café where he turned his travel planning prowess to finding tickets that wouldn't completely destroy us.

* * *

Back in Singapore, the kids and I were awake and eager to find out whether or not we could continue on our journey. Our first order of business was to find breakfast that cost less than the Crowne Plaza's exorbitant rate of $90 for a plate of eggs.

Thankfully, there was a McDonalds at the opposite end of the terminal where, after telling my oldest to 'come on' at least seven thousand times, we found not just breakfast but a nice Irish family with kids who wanted to play. They very kindly asked if I needed any money – I declined but I deeply appreciated the offer. We also found a lovely Chinese lady who thought all the children needed balloons and half a dozen computers with free internet.

Even better, my husband had found us flights and he only needed our passport details to book them. I had resourcefully thought to bring the passports along in case I needed to book flights on my own, so within an hour, we had all the relevant information we needed to fly on.

We would continue from Singapore to Perth that afternoon and then from Perth to Melbourne the following morning. Of course, that was at 11.00 in the morning, an hour before we had to be out of our room. We wouldn't be able to collect our boarding passes till at least 4.00 in the afternoon.

Eager to get on with it already, I stopped into a small shop for diapers and juice boxes, checked out of our hotel, loaded up a luggage trolley and set off for the tram that would take us to the departures area where we could check in and pick up our boarding passes.

If I'd been even a smidge less fervent to be on my way, it would have occurred to me exactly how little the departures area would have to offer in the way of entertainment while we waited four long hours to check in.

Other than one coffee shop, three hundred disconsolate travelers, one full gaggle of Chinese women who doted on the boys without speaking a word of English and three soldiers who marched through the terminal in formation carrying AK-47s, there wasn't much to see.

Though my oldest was full of energy, my youngest was bored enough by it all to fall asleep in my arms. I was able to prepare a makeshift pallet on the floor for him out of my sweater and his jacket, complete with a pillow fashioned from the package of diapers.

A more diligent mother might define the floor of an international airport as 'dirty', but in light of the circumstances it looked 'clean enough' and even 'not that bad' to me. I mean, how was I supposed to watch over our luggage (which would be taken away and detonated if left unattended), carry a sleeping child and chase my toddler who was running laps around the departures gate at Olympic speed all at the same time?

I was so frazzled by the time we could check in that I found myself coveting other families whose children were safely strapped into prams. At one point, I clearly thought, and may have even said aloud, 'I would kill you and your whole family for that stroller right now.'

Silent or articulate, I must have been wearing the same sort of twitchy expression a serial killer gets in the final moments before embarking on a shooting rampage because, as soon as the other passengers realized that it was *my* son lying with his face resting directly on the floor, finally playing quietly with his truck after hours of giving chase, they stopped making snarky comments.

Once we'd cleared the check-in counter and made it into the departures lounge, we discovered a play area complete with a climbing frame, slides, sinks, toilets and a TV with cartoons in English which we were able to enjoy for exactly one hour. Still, with any luck, the boys would run themselves into the ground and then sleep a goodly portion of our next flight.

* * *

As it turned out, luck was not on my side. In fact, Luck had sent his famous cousin Misfortune and the lesser known You've Got to Be Kidding Me to take his place.

The flight from Singapore to Perth, while a very good price, was on one of Australia's budget airlines. The ticket price was low because the airline hadn't wasted money on supplying the planes with TVs, movies or entertainment of any kind. There was nothing whatever to amuse my children for the duration of the six-and-a-half-hour flight but one meager aisle that ran down the middle of two rows of seats.

And with the exception of 45 short minutes, neither child slept the entire way.

I was only able to survive the journey by joining forces with the only other mom on the flight. She watched my oldest entertain her daughter in their seats while I chased my youngest up and down the aisle, a good deal both ways.

Between the two of us, we were able to withstand the impenetrable cloud of hatred emanating from the other passengers who were mostly younger travelers, backpackers and students who are willing to forgo the comforts of full-fare flights in order to afford flights at all. Budget travelers, as it turns out, are perhaps less patient with screaming toddlers than any other travelers in the world.

At one point, towards the end of the flight when the whole adventure was thoroughly worn through, my youngest launched into a squall of Biblical proportions. All I could do was wrestle his tantrum, containing it to our three seats. I could hardly blame him, but then I'm his mother and knew all he'd been through in the previous 48 hours.

Try though they might, the six college-aged boys in the two rows behind us couldn't keep the looks of unadulterated loathing from their faces. One particularly loud screech and all twelve eyes rolled onto me at once. Since I had their attention, I thought I should seize the teachable moment.

'Let this be a lesson to you boys,' I quipped, nearly dropping my bizarrely strong son as he flailed in my arms. To their credit, none of the college boys told me where I could stick my lesson, but I could see all of them taking mental inventory of their wallets, checking for condoms.

* * *

We arrived in Perth at last, where I barely kept the kids in check waiting for our luggage. No one would help me but then why would they? Every other passenger on our flight hated us with a passion known only to middle school teachers and terrorists. The other mother might have spared me some sympathy if she hadn't had her own equally big fish to fry.

As it was, when my oldest asked if he could ride in the stroller, I announced in my too-loud American voice that I would pay a million dollars for a stroller at that moment. I am sorry to say that the F word made an appearance in that sentence, to the shock and horror of every other passenger within earshot – except for the other mother.

She laughed in sympathy but clung nervously to her own stroller lest I pry it from her grip.

As my first stop coming into the country, I had to clear customs in Perth. There, one bag of M&Ms cost me perhaps the longest hour of my life. In the US, customs agents roam the arrivals hall with German Shepherds looking for drugs and weapons. In Australia, they bring beagles looking for fruit. How can you take a country seriously when their idea of intimidation is Snoopy bouncing around with a good natured wag of his tail?

I stood in line tired, hungry, thirsty and thoroughly annoyed. I'd brought enough food, juice and water to keep the kids placated for the duration of the flight, but I had only had one swallow of water to spare for myself the entire way.

The last straw finally broke when I learned I had to take a bus from the international terminal to the domestic terminal from which we'd take the last leg of our flight. I didn't mind the idea of taking the bus – what I minded was the surly bus driver who demanded $8 for the ride.

Thankfully the kids were finally running out of puff. They were content to sit still while I loaded the big suitcase, the full backpack and an unwieldy package of diapers onto the bus under the watchful and thoroughly useless eye of the driver who didn't so much as budge from his seat to help me. When I handed him a $100 note, he looked down his nose with a smirk.

'You'll have to get change,' he condescended in a voice that made me truly hate the Australian accent for the first time in my life.

I scooped up the children and the backpack with our money and passports to storm back into the airport. When the driver suggested I leave my children on the bus, I snarled.

'They're *one* and *three*. I'm not leaving them on this *bus* with *you*.'

The cute, young boy at the money changing kiosk inside the airport had no idea he'd just taken up a tiger's tail when I approached. He was a typical looking Aussie surfer type with blonde hair and blue eyes, probably working for beer money.

All he said was 'tough flight?' but it was enough to unleash all the tears that had been building up since Singapore.

I bawled out a brief rundown of my woes, starting with missing our first two standby flights and ending with a description of the hateful bus driver that included the F word in all its various grammatical forms. By the end, I was speaking in sentence fragments punctuated with heaving tears.

'...and now (sob!) the driver (sob!) won't take my money (sob!)...'

The poor surfer boy sat stiffly through my tirade with the slack jawed, blank stare of a dog watching television. He didn't break his eye contact with me once, not even as he made change and replaced my last few Singapore dollars with Australian ones.

His quick glance at the kids confirmed that he must have been thinking: 'I really *must* stop for condoms on the way home.'

All things considered, the kids had been as good as could possibly be expected. The oldest had done exactly what I'd asked of him nineteen times out of every twenty, the youngest maintained his mild, slightly startled expression most of the time and no one had diarrhea or vomiting.

On the bus between the Perth airport terminals, the three of us carried on an elaborate discussion involving airplanes and street lights, and we were all pretty sure we saw a dragon. Despite all the miles and misery, the kids managed to heal me as kids are so often able to do.

* * *

At last, we arrived at Perth's nearly empty domestic terminal to wait for our next flight. I gave in to tittering hysterics for about 90 seconds too long when I found a rank of at least 150 free strollers. My oldest astutely observed, 'Everybody isn't here' and no wonder – it was 1.00 in the morning and our final flight didn't leave for another five and a half hours.

While the boys raced each other, taking it in turns to test drive every single stroller on the premises unmolested, I used the automatic machines to check in and secure the last two side-by-side seats on our flight. All I would need to do when the gate agents arrived the next morning was drop off our bags.

With so much time on our hands and all reserves of energy completely exhausted, we had plenty of time to sleep. There was one perfect spot, a single row of six chairs without armrests, but this prime real estate was conveniently taken up by one kindly man who told me how cute my children were then stretched himself out to full length, taking up every inch of the seats.

He watched without comment, reclining himself on the padded comfort of the seats, while I dipped into our gigantic suitcase to make a bed on the floor from sweaters and jackets. Two soft packing cubes stuffed full of underwear made perfect pillows. My mood restored, I couldn't even see the point in killing the guy, now snoozing on the seats.

Once the kids were asleep, I thought it would be best if I tried to get some rest myself. I'd been awake for so many consecutive hours I couldn't even count them anymore. Tucking the passports, tickets and money underneath me, I curled up on the floor beside the kids. I was half hoping thieves would steal the suitcase. Other than the gifts we'd brought for the family, I couldn't have cared less if I ever saw the damn thing again.

I had just closed my eyes and started my descent into sleep when I heard a pair of sandals flip flop by. On the edge of sleep, I heard the flips flop, then pause, then flip again.

I opened my eyes to find myself making meaningful eye contact with another, (slightly) less common type of Aussie bloke. This forty-plus year old surfer had naturally blonde hair that he'd most likely dreadlocked the hard way through 25 years of chasing waves, smoking pot and sleeping on the beach. He was staring directly into my eyes, but as soon as he saw me looking at him, he flip flopped away. He was *probably* harmless.

Just like the water at the house in Cudgee *probably* didn't carry amoebic dysentery.

Suddenly I found I wasn't that tired anymore. Instead of sleeping, I got up, regrouped and packed away everything but the bare essentials for the morning flight.

Just as I settled down with a book, up rocked another beachcomber, this one dark haired and rangy bearded, reeking of booze. While I considered moving my children into the ladies restroom, Crazy Beard told me in a voice loud enough to be heard over Grand Central Station that my kids were cute and were they sleeping?

No, I thought to myself, I've bludgeoned them both to death, which is why they're lying still with their eyes closed breathing through their mouths at 2.00 in the morning.

'Yes,' I stage whispered, trying to impress on the smelly man both the need for quiet and my willingness to bludgeon *him* to death if he woke them. He thankfully passed out but not before taking off his shoes and setting them two inches away from the head of my oldest son, who had the sense to roll over in his sleep. I spent the rest of the night reading and watching over the kids as they mercifully, mercifully sleep.

* * *

At sunrise, all was OK. As soon as the gate agents arrived, I was able to check the bags while the kids slept. We made it through to our gate with the impending sense of relief one feels at their first glimpse of the light at the end of the tunnel.

Another hour and it was time to board the Qantas domestic which was full to the gills. My oldest was happy to watch the clouds go by and play quietly while my youngest slept soundly on my lap.

We arrived in Melbourne nearly four hours later, strangely calm, like the survivors of a hurricane or a Macy's last of season sale. I lugged my little one on my hip all the way to baggage claim while his brother contently held my hand, neither the worse for the wear after their night spent on the airport floor. When I saw my husband running across the parking lot to meet us, I nearly wept with relief.

He hadn't been lying in a bed of roses himself. After booking our flights, he'd flown from Brisbane to Melbourne then driven three hours to his parents' house in Warrnambool the night before and was now back to pick us up and drive the same three hours *again*.

He would have been driving for nine of the last twenty hours by the time it was all said and done. Still, I didn't have a lot of patience for him when the first words out of his mouth were, 'Man, that jump seat flight was a killer!'

I was too stunned to speak, which was probably a good thing.

* * *

In the end, we got our Instant Karmic Refund on the way back home. We got on the direct standby flight from Melbourne to Abu Dhabi on our first try, and the flight was so empty that we had eight seats between the four of us.

Even better, my husband regained my everlasting love and appreciation on the last six hours of the fourteen-hour journey. He stood watch over the boys while I stretched out over three seats and had as restful a sleep as you can get in economy class.

All my husband was left to do was watch movies, drink red wine and reassure himself that flying standby wasn't so bad after all.

FAIRIES

Every December, I develop a guilt complex when it comes time to tell my children that a fat, old man is going to fly all around the world in one night bringing toys to every child on the planet via a sleigh pulled by reindeer.

My five year old can't make sense of the physics. The sleigh would have to be huge to carry that many toys, but a giant airplane can only hold a certain number of people so how could eight tiny reindeer manage to pull a piece of machinery that by all rights shouldn't be able to achieve liftoff without the engines of an A380?

He does, however, understand that if he doesn't stop hitting his brother and get into the bath *right this minute*, Santa Claus isn't going to bring him any presents. I cringe every time I say the words, but that line only works between the 20th and the 24th of December, so I've got to get out of it what mileage I can.

I'd go the route of some practical parents and keep the myths to a minimum, but I'm reminded of the night I first watched *Peter Pan* on television when I was maybe six years old.

In a heroic act of bravery, Tinkerbell drank the poison intended for Peter, flying between his lips and the bottle without a second of hesitation. As she lay dying, Peter shocked us down to our days-of-the-week panties when he looked directly into the camera and told us to clap our hands if we believed in fairies.

It was as if he was actually talking to me, but neither of my sisters nor I believed that clapping would make a difference. Hadn't my mother told me a thousand times that what we see on television is make-believe? Hadn't she said that I should stop imagining things and pay attention to the real world? So when Tinkerbell took that mortal blow, there was nothing we could do but cry.

Until, that is, my mother said, 'Well, girls! Clap!' in a tone of voice that suggested that doing anything less was just ridiculous.

That was all it took. If my mother believed in fairies – my mother who gave us vitamins and broccoli and butter-free popcorn, the most sensible person on the face of the Earth – then maybe clapping would save Tinkerbell. So we clapped furiously and by a miracle, Tinkerbell heard us and was saved.

A stricter mother might call it 'lying', but if you can't believe in fairies when you're six, when can you?

Naked in the Driveway

* * *

My mom was right in encouraging me to pay attention to the world around me, though. I've gotten better as I've aged, but even as an adult I don't always notice the things I should.

One of the first things I did when I arrived in Abu Dhabi was join a gym. I'd run my second marathon just a couple of weeks before I left the US and was determined to stay true to my fitness regime.

After a few strenuous weeks in Abu Dhabi, though, I fell in with a sociable crowd and started giving my iron-pumping work-outs a miss in favor of dinners out with my friends and all-you-can-eat weekend brunches. Eventually, I realized that I hadn't been to the gym in months, my ass was getting huge and it was high time to take matters in hand.

My first day back on the work-out wagon, I dressed for the gym at home and took my street clothes with me. In my hurry to get started, I dropped my bag in a corner of the weight room rather than getting a locker.

In my absence, the gym had undergone some major renovations including new exercise machines and a whole separate work-out room for women upstairs. Content to stick with the familiar and get inspiration looking at sweaty, muscled-up men, I chose the co-ed gym downstairs.

After a good hard work-out, I rushed to my favorite spot in the change room to strip out of my spandex gear and take a shower. My first thought upon entering the dressing room was that it was trashed. There were clothes everywhere – on the floor, in piles on the bench. It was a real mess.

'Geez!' I thought to myself as I kicked off my shoes and pulled my dank t-shirt over my head. 'These women are slobs!'

I was down to shorts and a sports bra and I was only seconds away from making that last heaving tug to pull the tight top over my head when, to my surprise and horror, a man walked into the dressing room.

WTF? I thought to myself.

'What are you doing in here?' I shouted at him, shooing him towards the door. 'This is the ladies' change room!'

'No – is men's change room,' said the man. He was clearly flustered by having caught me in such an advanced state of undress, and he couldn't seem to find the right words in what was clearly his second language.

I wasn't buying it. I *knew* I was in the same room I'd always used before. This guy was some sort of pervert and...

About the same time, I noticed the crisp, long white khandura robe hanging on a hook with a red and white checked keffiyeh head scarf and black rope-like agal beside it – all the traditional garb of *men* from the Gulf region. The intruder sheepishly held open the door and pointed to the huge sign that I'd missed:

Naked in the Driveway

'Men's change room. Ladies change room has been moved upstairs.'

I'd actually put my hand on the sign to open the door and still hadn't seen it.

What. An. Idiot.

* * *

After almost being arrested for indecency, it was awhile before I went back to the gym. The good news, though, is that I've started working out again. Earlier this year, I started a fitness regime for the New Year – my personal trainer has taken me under his wing and promised that if I work hard and eat better, I can lose enough weight that people will stop asking me if I'm pregnant.

It's a pretty flimsy fitness goal, I know, but an important one.

It seems like I've spent the last 30 years thinking I was fat. The day I graduated high school, I weighed 105lbs (about 51kg) but when I looked in the mirror before slipping into my purple robe, all I saw was the cellulite on my thighs and a roll of neck fat.

I'm hoping my fitness program will get me back down to the weight I was when I was breastfeeding my youngest son, a weight even less than what I was the day I got married. But even in the days when I was single and that magical number registered on the scale every day, I still thought I was fat.

However fat I am right now, though, if I were to gain another 30lbs, I'd wish with all my heart that I could go back to the weight I am today, which means that however good or bad I *actually* look is all down to perception.

Turns out the true secret to aging well is to really let yourself go in your youth. Until you turn 35 years old, set the bar nice and low. Don't worry about high heels and facial treatments and make-up. When you're young, youth itself is all you need to look good. Sure, you can make an effort and look even better, but you'll want to save those big guns for when you really need them.

Instead of wishing I could look younger, what I need to do is take a good long look at my face and figure out what's going to blow out next. I know a lot of women my age with way more wrinkles around their eyes, uneven skin tone, acne and liver spots on their hands. Instead of bemoaning what's gone wrong, I should be celebrating what hasn't happened yet.

Because – as sure as the sun will rise – that day is coming.

* * *

Though I haven't deteriorated as much as I'm eventually bound to, I still wouldn't call myself photogenic – unlike my children, both of whom the camera loves. I recently got around to ordering my son's violently expensive school photos from last year, and I'm still in a tiff about it.

After his picture day, instead of the old-fashioned paper order form, I got a link to a website where I found over a dozen fantastic shots of my adorable youngest son. He looks like an actual child model, one who could persuade people the world over to buy everything from diapers to organic applesauce to cars with expensive safety features. The photos cost so much, however, that I can only afford a few tiny shots, all of which must be given to friends and family.

It makes me hate the talented photographer.

The guy I really like is the one who shot my older son's school pictures. This guy photographed an entire school full of kids wearing red shirts against a background of day-glow green. Even better, he managed to capture my otherwise handsome firstborn son mid-gawk.

These pictures were even worse than my son's very first batch of school photos when he entered nursery school in which he was clearly in the middle of telling a joke when they snapped the shot.

I especially love the class photo. Unlike all the other kids who are staring with vacant eyes into the distance, my son is covering his mouth in the middle of a giggle. I'll take grin of the devilish imp over the 1000 yard stare, but I think I have a few interesting years ahead of me.

This year he's in kindergarten and for a very reasonable amount of cash that I stapled to the form and returned via his backpack, I now have several copies of that one terrible shot of my kid, enough to give away to every person I've ever met. It's the first in the arsenal of photos I can use to threaten him with in the future.

'If you start smoking,' I can say in a few years' time, 'I'm putting your school photos in your wedding montage!'

Thanks to his photographer, when my oldest son grows up to be as gorgeous as his father, he can look back at that bad picture (and all the others that are sure to come after it) and think to himself, 'I've known suffering – I used to look like that.'

Because unless you're actually a professional child model, that's what school photos are for.

* * *

Unfortunately, it seems all the other mothers prefer to spend an inordinate amount of money for a handful of my-kid-could-be-a-model shots. These are the mothers I worry about.

In the course of my career as a writer, I've researched a huge variety of parenting issues, everything from sleep struggles to temper tantrums to biting. Usually I learn plenty of tips I can incorporate myself, but I came across one disorder a couple of years ago that made me feel even more insecure as a mother.

Which I kind of thought wasn't really possible.

Apparently there's an entire disorder called 'hurried child syndrome' which happens when kids are so heavily booked with after-school activities and lessons that they develop stress-related illnesses.

The cure, I learned, was to allow children time for what the experts call 'unstructured play', the sort where the kids pick up non-electronic toys and play accordingly, preferably with other kids. When I wrote the article, I even had to include a how-to list of guidelines for conducting a session of unstructured play.

Seriously? Am I really in such a minority as a mother? Are there really that many other moms so eager to enrich their children that they go overboard? My children are masters of unstructured play - I call it, 'Mommy is working! Go play! I have things to do!'

In fact, my children have been known to get on their tricycles and announce that they're going to the office to work. They'll mimic typing and pretend to answer the remote control, saying 'Hello - Laura Fulton'.

When do these other over-achieving, activity-booking, creativity-stimulating mothers cook dinner or take a shower? Personally, I can't tell you how many words I've written while in the act of breastfeeding, with a kid on my lap, saying 'just a minute' or 'get it yourself'. It's not often I have to say, 'If you boys don't keep it down, I'm going to put you both out in a box by the street'.

But it's happened.

The good news is that, by leaving my children to 'stimulate' themselves and allowing them plenty of 'unstructured play', they've learned how to do all kinds of things including prepare a bowl of cereal, change into super hero costumes and evenly distribute the crumbs of two pieces of toast evenly over both the sofa *and* the love seat.

Can't learn *that* in an afterschool activity.

* * *

While I'm very likely to tell my kids to bugger off so I can work, I'd like to think they still feel loved. In fact, every so often, I worry that I'm spoiling my children.

Take the recent trip I took with the kids to New York City. In preparing the boys for the visit, I'd told them about all the things we would do while we were there, including visiting the massive three-story Toys R Us in Times Square where I'd promised they could each pick out one toy.

For weeks in advance, the boys discussed which toy they would get. While my oldest agonized at length, my youngest knew straight away what he wanted – Superman. At the tender age of three, my baby knows that, no matter what powers any other super hero might possess, Superman will always be the superior hero. Case closed.

He's a purist – and he's right. Superman kicks all other asses. I love him for that.

As it turns out, there was only one Superman action figure in the whole multilevel store. It was the perfect size and came complete with plastic hair and a real cape made of fabric, but he was only available as part of a three-piece set that cost $27.

Seriously? $27? Still, when I asked my dear sweet baby son what he wanted, Superman was the only thing he asked for. Since one of the other figures in the set was a Batman (also with a fabric cape, suitable for flapping in the wind) I figured it would be money well spent. Besides, could I really say no after so many weeks?

Now, some kids will get a toy, play with it for five minutes and then forget all about it. Not my kids, especially my youngest – if I give him a toy he really likes, he'll play with it for days on end, incorporating it into every game.

Thus Superman entered out lives, coming with us to every meal, sitting at attention as we watched a video about the city that never sleeps, taking in the view from the top of the Empire State Building, gazing up at the Statue of Liberty with respect.

On the last day of our trip, it took us two trains, a bus and a three-block walk through the Bronx to get to the city's most famous zoo. After an unseasonably warm afternoon spent walking and admiring all the animals with Superman, it was time for the three-block walk back to the bus.

With one toy in hand apiece, the kids carried on like champions, walking without complaining the entire way. As soon as we were on the bus, though, my youngest fell asleep. Unsure about where we needed to disembark, I finally got off the bus with my little one asleep in my arms.

It wasn't until we arrived back at our hotel room that I realized he'd dropped the faithful Superman in his sleep on the bus and, in my distraction, I hadn't noticed.

Of course, my youngest son was distraught, and in all fairness it wasn't his fault. He's only three years old, after all. So as soon as we got to my sister's house in Arkansas, we went to Wal-Mart where I found the same Superman in the same three-piece set, this time at the discounted price of $20.

After a few days of debate, I finally broke down and bought the second Superman and my baby son has been delighted ever since. In fact, he had his second Superman in his hand a week later when I saw the very same set marked down to $13.

The good news is that the second Superman made it home through a series of unfortunate events that included missed flights, mechanical airplane failures and an unexpected overnight stay in Minneapolis. Cape a-flapping, he's still my son's favorite toy.

Man of steel, indeed.

* * *

Though I ended up spending almost $50 for The Most Expensive Superman on the Face of the Earth, I'm not usually so loose with money. This past weekend, with the idea of saving a little cash, I bought electric hair clippers. My oldest son went to school with a little friend last year who had a simple buzz cut and it was really cute, so when I asked my son if he liked his friend's hair and did he want to look the same, he said sure.

Now, having spent as much as $10 apiece in the past on haircuts for the boys, I figured even I could pull off a buzz cut by myself. I mean, how hard can it be? I've watched the barber at work plus I've seen plenty of military movies with scenes of young soldiers getting their heads shaved. As long as I leave the guard in place, it's just a matter of running the clippers over the entire head, right?

My oldest went first, excited to try something new and happy to appease his mother. The guard that determines the length of the hair that gets left behind goes as high as 'ten' so I set it at 'five', thinking if I got it a little too long on the first go around, I could always cut it shorter later.

Turns out 'five' is about a millimeter longer than what new recruits in the Marines get. Thankfully, my oldest son was very pleased with his new haircut and trotted away happy.

Having not seen his brother's new look, my little one climbed dutifully up onto the stool and let me buzz away. He didn't turn around to look at himself until I was finished – at which point he burst into tears.

'Mommy, where is my hair?' he wailed. 'I don't want my hair gone! Put it back!'

After a few frantic moments of picking up handfuls of hair off the bathroom floor, he accepted that the strands were not going to stick back onto his head and he simply wept.

In truth, he did look a little like a convict on a ship bound for Australia. More accurately, he looked exactly like photos I've seen of my dad from 1950 when he was a little boy about the same size my kids are right now and very cute – an observation on my part that did exactly nothing to console my son.

OK, OK. I've learned my lesson. Next time I'll turn the guard up to 'seven'.

* * *

Despite the classic haircuts my kids are sporting, I'm not usually so old-fashioned. I'd go so far as to say I'm pretty hip, down with the youth culture, even.

Last night, for example, I was sweating away at the gym – climbing an endless flight of stairs on the StepMill – when one of my favorite songs at the moment came on the radio, the duet between rapper Eminem and Caribbean beauty Rihanna.

Through the miracle of the iPhone app TuneIn Radio, I was listening to Capital FM, a popular mainstream station that broadcasts from London. I'd just switched over from the French hip hop station out of Paris, not in the mood for the Spanish rap station that's based in the Dominican Republic.

As the song played, whole lines scrambled into a musical blur so that, even though I knew the lyrics, I couldn't hear the words. In fact, every reference to violence or anger had been edited out of the song.

Now, I've lived in Abu Dhabi for a long time and I'm used to hearing songs that have been edited for content. As much as I'm a strong believer in the freedom of speech, I can understand why a UK station would feel compelled to downplay references to violence in light of the recent riots.

When I was 25, I would have been deeply offended by having the lyrics of a song diluted for unsavory content. I would have argued that I was a responsible adult, able to hear those references and make decisions for myself.

Now that I have children, though, I get it.

I mean, I can hardly turn on the radio these days without hearing a song that glorifies drinking to excess and making poor decisions based on borderline alcoholism, the sort that lead to unplanned pregnancy and parental gray hair.

As I write, preteens around the world are doing a Google search for ménage à trois, thinking they need to have one for their Friday night to be complete. And a big fat thank you for THAT, Katie Perry. (At least they'll learn how to spell ménage à trois – I just did.)

And it's not just Miss Perry. We have Lady Gaga singing about being so drunk she's lost her phone and Ke$ha brushing her teeth with Tennessee whiskey. Seriously? I mean, why go with that redneck swill when there's perfectly good single malt scotch on offer? And talk about a bad influence...

Oh. Oh no. There it was. That was it, right there, three paragraphs ago. I just turned into my mother. Well, shit. Can somebody please pass the Glenlivet?

* * *

For all the time I have to spend in the gym to stay fit, it seems to come naturally to my kids. Last night, instead of getting dressed for bed, my youngest son bypassed his pajamas and went straight for his Superman costume. Not to be fussed with the entire ensemble, he contented himself with just the cape and nothing else.

Seeing my three year old running – no, flying – around the house naked but for a red cape, I was struck by just how sturdy he is. Seriously, I haven't seen muscle tone like that since I was sightseeing in New York City and saw the handsome young Abercrombie and Fitch models standing outside the shop on Fifth Avenue wearing nothing but board shorts. (And let me tell you what a buffet for the eyes *that* was, my friends.)

My little guy is a true toughie, but then he sort of has to be to survive living with my firstborn – but not because of any sibling rivalry. Even though my youngest usurped his brother's position as Only Child, the older one has never harbored any ill will against his brother.

When the little one was a baby, his brother would give him Matchbox cars. The oldest was delighted that his infant brother was able to clutch the hand-sized race cars and took the baby's gripping reflex as a sign of a mutual admiration for all vehicles, both shiny and matte.

One day I needed to do a bit of housework, so I strapped the little one in his infant swing, setting the automatic mechanism at level three. When I came back ten minutes later, I found him wide eyed, swinging on level ten as fast as the machine would go and clutching the guard rail for dear life.

'Mommy, look!' squealed his older brother. 'I put it on fastest! He likes it!'

While the baby wasn't laughing, he also wasn't crying or throwing up. So maybe he did like it. He also didn't seem to mind all the times I left him sleeping and came back to find him awake thanks to his brother 'papping' his head and kissing him.

Now that he's old enough to have a vote in what movie we're going to watch or what we'll have for dinner, the little one is still content to go along with his older brother – who milks that support for all it's worth.

'We want to watch *The Incredibles*, don't we?' I'll hear my oldest say. 'We don't want carrots, do we?'

Of course, the little one always agrees.

But while he's happy to go along with what his brother wants a lot of the time, I'm not worried about my baby. He's tough enough to stick up for himself – he *has* to be if he's going to survive his big brother's rough and tumble love.

* * *

OK, fellow mothers, exactly who do we think we're kidding with Nutella? They call it 'hazelnut spread', like it should belong in the peanut butter family. Ha! You can put it in the breakfast foods aisle all you want. It still looks exactly like cake frosting to me.

If we're going to call Nutella a sandwich spread – an actual food rather than a dessert – then I'm going to start feeling a lot better about myself. I mean, there's got to be at least 9000 calories in every tablespoon.

Thankfully, my vision is starting to fail me so I can't read the label, even on the big jar I recently bought, and I'm not about to Google it or look it up on the über-handy calorie counter app I just downloaded onto my iPhone. Personally, I'd really rather not know.

Considering what an incredibly bad mother I've consistently been over the course of the last five years, it's sort of amazing that I only bought my very first jar of Nutella this past week. It's not a spread I grew up eating (I had a good mother) and, since it's nut-based, it's not one I can put in the kids' lunchboxes.

In fact, I might have never wandered down the hazelnut path if I hadn't discovered that my sister – who is a *way* better mother than I am – gives Nutella to her highly intelligent son, so it *must* be OK. Even so, as I stand in my kitchen slathering chocolaty 'goodness' (ha!) all over a frozen waffle that's just spent 30 seconds in the microwave, it seems wrong somehow.

The only real health benefit of Nutella, I think, is that now that my kids have both acquired a taste for it, I can insist they each eat a piece of fruit before they can belly up to the breakfast bar for another choco-waffle. My kids are breathless enough for another bite of our new found 'nutritious' (ha!) nut spread, in fact, that I think I could get them to do just about anything.

Come to think of it, Nutella is actually very good for them. Yep - definitely healthy.

* * *

Though I've stopped feeling bad about feeding my kids Nutella, I've had to get way more serious about what I eat myself. Shockingly, the New Year's Resolution I made months ago to lose weight has really been hanging in there.

Even a recent trip to see my family barely put a dent in my fitness/diet plan for post-baby skinniness. Even better, my husband has gotten onboard and has put the full force of his considerable resolve towards creating a healthy lifestyle for the two of us, cooking healthy meals and sticking with exercising.

I tell you, the flab on my thighs doesn't know what's hit it.

In keeping with our regime, we went to the gym last night to get a few calories in reserve to offset the ones we were about to consume at dinner with friends. Hoping to get the most bang for my buck, I climbed up onto the most evil machine in the gym's arsenal - the StairMill.

In the StairMaster family, this particular torture device is meant to punish in increments over a period of time rather than getting it over and done with all at once. The mechanical staircase just keeps revolving and revolving until you develop the sense to get off.

Determined to burn enough calories so I could have an indulgent dinner, I pulled on my hot pink tennis skort and matching hot pink tank top, climbed to the top of the mill and started stepping.

Now, the way the machine is designed, a mini staircase of about six steps revolves sort of like a waterwheel so rather than just moving my feet up and down like on the old fashioned stepper, I have to actually pick up my feet and climb. With so many stairs to accommodate, the machine towers high above all the rest of the equipment in the gym. Climbing aboard, I knew that people couldn't help but look at me.

Still, I *was* wearing my cute pink work-out gear and I *have* lost a considerable amount of weight since the first of the year, so – I thought with confidence – let 'em look. I'm about as smoking hot as I'm ever likely to be again in this lifetime.

My confidence was confirmed when I caught one of the gym's personal trainers checking me out. He's a good looking guy, and even if he is young enough to be my own son (provided I'd gotten pregnant in university), it was nice to have him looking.

'Better watch it, cowboy,' I thought to myself. 'See that big guy on the verge of having a heart attack over there on the exercise bike? That's my husband and he's a jealous man. I haven't seen him in a fist fight in awhile, but let him cool down and catch his breath and he could Kick. Your. Ass. So try not to be too obvious with the staring.'

Validated, I kicked up the intensity a couple of levels and powered through the rest of my work-out, noticing every single time the man/boy stole a glance at me. I was basking, in fact, in the glow of his admiration when I climbed off the StairMill and went to check in with my husband.

'Are you OK?' Sweating from the hard session on the bike he'd just finished, my beloved stopped panting as soon as he saw me.

'Yeah - why?' I asked, hands on jaunty hips.

'Look at your face.'

If there's a name for the color my face goes when I work out really hard, I don't know what it is. I do know that the shade in question is somewhere between fuchsia and burgundy and that, even when I'm done exercising, it stays that color for awhile.

Stud Muffin probably didn't think I was 'hot' but rather actually, literally hot - he was probably keeping an eye on me and wondering at what stage he should call an ambulance, bless his young, athletic heart.

Gotta' love a comprehensive reality check.

* * *

Speaking of reality checks, one of my girlfriends is pregnant with her first child, and I asked her recently if the baby was going to be a boy or a girl.

'I don't know,' she said with a dreamy smile. 'I want it to be a surprise.'

OK, seriously? Let me tell you, sister, there are so many surprising things about having your first baby that the child's gender doesn't really need to be one of them.

For starters, you won't believe exactly how long it takes for your waters to break. In the movies it's just one big splash – in reality, it can go on for hours and hours. Literally. The rest of childbirth is so comprehensively gross we won't get into it here. Suffice it to say that you will spend the majority of your labor and delivery shocked to shit.

And that's just giving birth.

For a lot of new mothers, it comes as a huge surprise the pure volume of human waste a tiny baby can produce. When you start calculating the amount of what goes in compared to what's coming out, the physics will seem impossible. And don't get me started on the smell – it can sear the tissue right off your corneas.

When I was pregnant, I wanted as few surprises as possible. I read all the books, I asked a million questions and I wanted to know the gender as soon as I could.

With both of my children, none of it seemed real until I knew who was in there. At that point, my baby developed an identity, preferences and opinions. I would read their horoscopes and I had lengthy conversations with my fetuses, especially in the car – we discussed all kinds of things and let me tell you, no one is a better listener than a fetus.

Except perhaps a dog who makes eye contact.

But the main reason for finding out if it's going to be a boy or a girl is the presents. I was absolutely spoiled rotten during both of my pregnancies thanks in large part to my profession – I was still teaching at the time, and a vast majority of my high school students gave me gifts, all of which I found enormously helpful once the babies were born. In fact, all of my favorite baby clothes – the pieces I've saved as keepsakes and ones I reluctantly passed on – were gifts.

I say, if you want a surprise, wait until the baby is born and then count how many hours you have stay awake at one go.

That one will kick you right in the teeth, I promise.

CAVEMEN

I have nothing but respect for my mother but, as it turns out, she didn't actually know everything. Like every other marriage expert, she spent our girlhoods telling me and my sisters that we should marry someone we could talk to.

Here's the reality. Men don't want to talk. Not to us girls, anyway, not about anything *we* want to talk about. They might spend all day talking about football and fishing lures and cleats, but they're not really interested in your day or most of your feelings. It's not that they don't care – OK, well, it sort of is – but it's also that they're just not listening.

The ugly truth about life is that most men like pretty girls with big boobs and lax morals, so if you're fat or plain or hard to get, it really doesn't matter how smart or funny or interesting you are.

Naked in the Driveway

You can be as eligible as you want, but the fact is that finding The Guy isn't like getting a college degree or climbing a mountain. No amount of hard work on your part will guarantee his appearance. Although, ironically, if you screw up enough, you can be sure he *won't* want you if he ever *does* come strolling into your life.

Which makes sense but still sort of sucks, I think.

Turns out there is one thing you can do to try to ease the process. Instead of trying to find a man you can talk to, what you really want to find is one you don't mind looking at while he scratches himself.

I've learned the hard way that when it comes to communicating in a marriage, what you *don't* say is every bit as important as what you *do* say. At least half the time, 'communicating' means shutting up and not making that scathing remark you'd love to say, not prattling on when he just needs some quiet time.

Provided there's plenty of enthusiastic sex, most men will put up with most of the crap most women can dish out. So plan on picking your husband the same way he picked you – marry a guy you're pretty sure you won't mind having sex with for a long time.

And when you want to talk, call your mother.

* * *

I always thought my parents had a great relationship, and they did. There was gratitude between them and a fair division of labor. Dad went to work every day while Mom ran the domestic affairs and her own business from home. When I was a single girl, it seemed ideal.

Now that I'm married, however, I realize that my mother got screwed.

It never occurred to me to question why it was OK for my dad to spend certain weekends in a boat on a lake from sunup to sundown while Mom continued to look after us, cook, clean, iron, buy discount groceries with coupons she'd clipped from the newspaper and sew all of our clothes by hand.

If my parents enjoyed a fair division of labor that means that everything my mom did was labor, too. When did she get a weekend on a fishing boat? I'll tell you when – never.

The famous relationship author John Gray (of *Mars/Venus* fame) defines what women have always known: men need a cave. If they don't get time in their cave, they act like grouchy little children. Somehow it's just fine for a man to clam up and act sullen if he doesn't get time on his own, so of course he needs a cave.

But hey Dr Gray? Guess what – we *all* need a cave!

A foolish man might be inclined to suggest that his wife doesn't need to spend time in a cave because she's 'only' been home with the kids all week. If the cave is a metaphor for 'time away from the family', why is it that a man who's already been away from his family for 40 hours this week needs a break but his wife – who's been with the kids 24 hours a day, seven days a week – doesn't?

'It's not the kids,' a husband might say. 'I mean, for God's sake, it's only two kids. My mom had five.'

Yeah? Well, your mom got screwed, too. Just two and a half times more.

Of course a mother wants to spend time with her children. Many women make the choice to sacrifice what they must so that they can stay home with their children instead of pursuing a career.

But there's no denying that caring for a home and children is work. At any rate, we call it 'work' when we pay someone else to do it. And just because I enjoy my job doesn't mean I never need a break from it. Most men will agree that they enjoy sex but they need a break from that, too.

I'd like to say this to those husbands – if you think looking after children is such a relaxing vacation that moms never need a break from it, how about *you* look after the kids and I'll go to *my* cave. It's gorgeous in there, filled with soft rugs, coffee, gin mixed with tonic, my friends, the occasional yoga session and lovely ladies grooming my feet.

While most men will argue that they're fine with the division of labor, a lot of them conveniently forget about the equal division of leisure.

A man will go to work, sprint for the day, come home and put his feet up. In contrast, a mother will wake up with the kids at any hour of the night, feed them, clean them, dress them, take them to school, spend the morning working, retrieve the children, look after them all afternoon while at the same time cleaning the house, cooking, ironing and running errands, then feed the kids some more, prepare their lunches for tomorrow, clean them some more, read to them, stimulate them and get them off to bed.

And that's the routine all day, every day. Weekends and holidays are just words for 'more of the same'.

So if I decide to spend an hour in my cave while my kids are at school, bite me.

* * *

Thankfully, my husband was raised well, so we've been able to maneuver around many of the arguments that pick at other marriages. But that's partly down to where he comes from.

In all my years growing up in a small town in Arkansas, nestled in a range of puny hills smack in the middle of America, the most exotic place I could imagine was Australia. Since marrying my husband, I've learned that in many major respects, Australia is almost exactly like America, but one thing they have that melts hearts the world over is that fantastic accent.

The British will tell you that we Americans are barely speaking English at all – I suspect they're still bitter that we no longer show their Queen on our money – but the fact is that, as a nation, we do love the sound of language.

I particularly love the woman at a car rental company in Springdale, Arkansas, who was utterly charmed by my husband when he called her the summer before we were married.

After a ten-minute, long-distance explanation of why he needed to pay for my rental car with his credit card, all she could say was, 'I love the way you sound' only with her Arkansawyer accent, it came out sounding like, 'Ah luuuuuv the why you say-yound.'

There have been plenty of benefits to marrying a guy with an accent. After five years, we still haven't gotten around to the most basic marital arguments, like which of us spends the most money or who is the fattest.

No, we're too busy trying to decide whether we're shopping for 'pro-deuce' or 'prod-juice', whether that piece of meat is a 'fill-let' or a 'fee-lay', whether we're standing in the 'foy-your' or the 'foy-yah'. It may be a lifetime before we get around to who loves whom the most.

It's not all sunshine and roses, though. For every bit it sounds like we're speaking the same language, we still have moments when we need a quick translation.

How much, exactly, is much of a muchness? Apparently, it's the same amount as six of one or half a dozen of another, but the expression itself makes no sense. Neither do so many other Australianisms.

When the kids were mucking around in the backseat one day, my husband said the youngest was carrying on like a pork chop. Now, how exactly would a pork chop carry on? Crackling and popping a bit? And when you say 'biscuit', do you mean 'sort of like a cookie' or 'sort of like a scone'?

When describing the likely outcome of a series of steps, the final result is often something to do with Bob becoming one's uncle, as in, 'The kids have jetlag? All we need to do is give them a can of Coke to keep them awake during the day and then some Benadryl to put them to sleep at night and then Bob's your uncle.'

Who is this Bob, and how did he suddenly become my uncle?

For all the misunderstandings, I hope the differences between me and my Antipodean husband will help keep our relationship interesting long after the expiry date on which I might have begun to tire of one of my hometown men. All I can say to any girl swooning over Prince Charming because she likes the sound of the way he talks – beware.

You get over it.

* * *

For years, I've blamed Cinderella for indoctrinating young girls with the Prince Charming Will Save You method of life management. I recently watched the very first feature film Disney ever made, though, and I was reminded that it was actually Snow White who sang that someday her prince would come.

This was a girl who sold the myth that housework is fun, animals don't poop on clean floors, brunettes have more fun, old ladies are mean and it's perfectly appropriate for a single girl to live with seven strange men.

Naked in the Driveway

True, it was 1937 when *Snow White* first hit the big screen, so maybe times have changed. What Ms White *didn't* tell us is that housework makes your hands scaly and that once a cat sprays your bathroom, that aroma is there to stay.

In the final installment of the *Shrek* series, Fiona was the first to step up and warn little girls that sometimes you can wait years for a prince who never comes. Sometimes you have to save yourself, she says, because there's no guarantee Mr. Charming will ever come and storm your tower, slaying dragons and quoting sonnets.

Of course I'm one to talk, what with my handsome metaphorical prince and two little heirs to the family throne. It was on the very last chime of my biological clock, admittedly, but he finally showed up in all his armored glory, sword in hand and dead dragons in his wake.

If anything, Gentle Reader, I should remind you that in the original story of Snow White, she only survived the poisoned apple because it was lodged in her throat. Which means the thing that saved her was not – as Fiona would have us believe – true love's kiss, but the Heimlich maneuver.

I suppose if a girl is going to wait around for a guy, it should be one who knows her heart. Because if he can find that, he should be able to locate her diaphragm.

* * *

Though I now feel safe saying my husband knows my heart, I married him in large part because he was the tallest, best looking guy at the bar that New Year's Eve. That he turned out to be a great guy was (almost) an afterthought.

I've learned the hard way that when you hang your future happiness on the breadth of a man's shoulders, you're probably going to get stuck with certain characteristics you wouldn't find in more refined men.

Being the burly Australian type, my husband is practically incapable of taking a dirty dish to the sink. When I tried my hand at painting, his only observation was to insist I didn't hang my canvases in the lounge room 'or anywhere else people might see them'. When I was pregnant and got a bad haircut, he couldn't console me but only asked, 'What am I supposed to do? Lie and say I like it when I don't?'

I might have tried divorcing him on the grounds of putting empty ice cube trays back into the freezer only I'm pretty sure I'd never get that to fly with Reverend Thompson down at St Andrews Church.

But it turns out my original instincts were spot on.

For one, my husband has a natural ability to play just about every sport - if genetics are in our favor, at least one of our kids may end up supporting me in my old age as a professional athlete. He can't kill our food, but my sturdy man has demonstrated his hunter instincts in cutthroat battle with the entire ant population which has besieged our house.

And then we bought our first barbeque grill.

Naked in the Driveway

My husband is definitely a caveman, and that quality works to my advantage most when I put a pair of tongs in his hand and station him in front of an open flame where he can work magic with a nice cut of tenderloin.

Give him raw meat and fire and his inner Cro-Magnon responds like the humming string of a violin. I can practically see fresh hair growing on his knuckles. I guess any man who can cook my very favorite meal – leaving me to rest on the sofa with a glass of wine – can empty all the ice cube trays he wants.

* * *

In our carport, beside our barbeque grill stands our latest acquisition, a hand-me-down four-seat pedal car. It looks a bit like a go-kart but it's powered by pedaling like a bicycle. Since it's been at our house, it's seen a lot of action.

Though my boys aren't big enough to pedal the car themselves, all the kids in the neighborhood have given the contraption a go, delighting my kids at the same time.

When our good friends Geoff and Andrew came over for dinner last week, they were happy to give the children a whirl. These two grown men got that pedal car flying at speeds I was sure were going to end in tears and broken arms. My little guys, of course, loved it.

The speeds were enough, in fact, to deeply ingratiate our guests to our children. When dinner was served, our boys insisted on sitting next to Geoff and Andrew, and the kids didn't want to go to bed until the guys valiantly volunteered to read them their bedtime stories.

The boys were so impressed with Geoff and Andrew that the next morning, when my youngest came padding into my room to give me my daily wake-up cuddle, his first words were, 'Mommy, where are my extra daddies?'

Now, wouldn't that be nice?

If I could enlist the services of extra dads, I would have two of them entirely devoted to earning big salaries. Since those two would be tired from working, I would have a third dad whose job it would be to teach the kids their times tables, the proper way to tie knots and how to build camp fires.

With Dad Number Three so busy with the kids, I'd probably go ahead and get a fourth dad to fix broken things around the house and kill the bugs. Then Dad Number Five could spend all his time rubbing my feet and telling me I'm beautiful.

As it turns out, being a father is hard work. If it were easy, as the proverbial saying goes, they would let women and children do it.

* * *

'Do *not* touch the camera!' my father ordered sternly.

It was only the 43rd time he'd issued the same edict. I was 16 years old the summer before my junior year of high school was to start and my family were on a trek across the country from Arkansas to California, visiting friends and relatives and seeing sights along the way.

Naked in the Driveway

In addition to renting an enormous, cushy van for the trip, Dad had also bought a new camera with which to chronicle our odyssey, and he would be damned if he was going to allow anything to happen to it.

As we hurtled down Interstate 40 through the deserts of New Mexico, my dad held the camera at arm's length, snapping pictures through the passenger window while he drove. My mother, having wisely washed her hands of the camera, sat back out of his way.

In addition to Dad's admonitions that we touched the camera on pain of death, he also became obsessed with the car keys.

'*Don't* lock the keys in the van!'

As far as I was concerned, both the camera and the car keys were untouchable, like toxic waste or Barry Manilow cassette tapes. I kept a safe distance from them both, hoping to avoid the bloody punishment that was sure to befall anyone who clicked an unwilling photo or menacingly jingled the keys.

Throughout the Southwest, every stop was accompanied by Dad's steely glare, focused on each one of us in turn:

'Do *not* touch the camera! *Don't* lock the keys in the van!'

In avoiding the camera and the keys, I gave my dad no reason to single me out, but my luck ran out when we reached Los Angeles.

Neither of my sisters or I had ever seen the ocean, so when we pulled into LA, my dad drove directly to the nearest public beach before we even checked into our hotel. We were delirious with excitement. As we piled out of the van, Dad issued his usual death threat then turned on me.

'*Don't* lose your glasses!'

My sisters didn't need glasses and my mom wore contact lenses, so Dad and I were the only ones with vision at stake. Dad, luckily, had a safety net. He was wearing his brand new, scratch-resistant, wire-rimmed glasses, but he'd brought his old pair just in case. I had but one pair.

'If you lose your glasses in the ocean,' he glowered, 'you'll just have to go blind for the rest of the trip.'

I was suitably terrified by the thought. When we reached the water's edge, still in shorts and t-shirts, I waded in only ankle-deep. I was so consumed, in fact, with watching my feet and holding my glasses firmly against my head that I didn't see the wave rise up and smack my father's face.

He had been bending beside my younger sister, pointing out something of aquatic interest on the ocean floor, when a bastard wave leapt up, snatched the glasses from his eyes and raced away with them. He floundered blindly for a moment and then stood, fists planted on his hips.

We all held our breath. What could we say? What would he do? After a moment of gazing contemplatively into the horizon, Dad looked around, shrugged and smiled with philosophical irony.

'The ocean claims all things,' he mused, and waved generally toward the sea.

A few days later, we pulled into the Disneyland parking lot, delirious with anticipation. We were all sunscreened and giddy, mapping out our plans for the day. Again, we piled out of our luxurious van. Our double side doors slammed shut. My mom's passenger door slammed shut. From the other side of the van, we heard Dad call.

'*Don't* touch the camera! *Don't* lock the keys in the...'

The slamming of his door was followed by a deathly, high-noon-at-the-OK-corral silence. We all froze. Mom sneaked a look through her window and then stifled a laugh as Dad rounded the van's front end, murder in his eyes.

On the console between the two front seats sat the keys, locked in the van by my dad's own hand.

After one quick conniption fit, he set about finding a solution. In a few minutes, he had yanked open the side doors just enough for my younger sister to reach through with her skinny arm and unlock the door.

Problem solved, Dad put on a cheery face. As we headed for the shuttle that would take us into the park, laughing with the relief of the recently condemned, we girls all said our silent prayers of thanksgiving that it hadn't been any of us who had committed the crime that turned out to be not such a big deal after all.

We spent the day enraptured with Disneyland. Even from the depths of my own adolescent angst, I was astounded by the number of surly Californian teenagers slinking around The Happiest Place on Earth like someone had just kicked each of them individually in the crotch.

'What could possibly be wrong with your life,' I wanted to ask them, 'that would inspire you to paint your fingernails black for a day out at Disneyland?'

For the remainder of the trip, Dad said nothing more about my glasses or the car keys. He still clung to the camera but was clearly loath to issue another warning.

Our last stop before heading back to Arkansas was the Redwood National Forest. We hiked through it, ate a picnic lunch and gaped at the enormous trees. One more restroom break and it was back to the van for the journey home. Returning from the ladies' room, Mom picked up the camera that had been left on the picnic table. With a gasp, Dad snatched it from her hands and stuffed it in his shirt pocket.

'*Don't* touch the camera! The last of our pictures are in there, including all the pictures from today!' he stormed. Turning his back on my mother's raised eyebrows, he stalked to the men's room.

My mother, in a testament to her patience, said nothing. My sisters and I all waited silently for our father's return, hoping at this point to avoid the attention of either of our parents.

After several moments, just when we had begun to wonder what Dad was doing in there, a low maniacal snigger began to echo from the men's room. The laughter rose, growing more and more hysterical. Finally, my father emerged holding the camera at arm's length.

He'd dropped it in a puddle on the floor where the film cover had popped open, exposing the last roll of film, but no further harm had been done. After one tense moment, we all giggled then laughed outright. From California back to Arkansas, Dad drove in mellow, sheepish silence.

He even let Mom take a picture.

* * *

Though my poor dad was saddled with three girls, I'm inclined to believe that great dads (like my husband) can produce great sons.

My oldest son, for example, is pretty brave for a five year old. He'll walk up to just about anyone and start a conversation, whether he speaks their language or not. He'll jump off the highest diving block into the deepest end of the swimming pool. He's been known to stand up to the class bully and make friends with a dog that outweighs him by over 100 pounds.

But when it comes to having his nails cut, his courage flies straight out the window.

Unlike his mother, who loves to see her feet properly groomed, my son lives in eternal terror of having his nails trimmed. No matter how gentle I am, he'll argue, scream, kick and plead.

Last night, once again, I had to bring out the clippers. We got through all ten fingers without one tear, but when it was time for the toes, he came unglued as usual. He went to school this morning, however, with lovely looking feet, thanks entirely to the efforts of my greatest hero, my husband.

For reasons I still don't fully understand, I managed to marry really well, probably better than I should have. My beloved has never shirked a day of work, he's way smarter than I am and my last nanny once asked me, 'Sir does not know how to yell?'

OK, he's not perfect. He'll take off his clothes in such a way that every garment remains connected (only wrong side out) and leave them in a pile on the floor. He firmly believes that he can brush his teeth, check his email and change his shirt all 'in five seconds'. He doesn't always respond well to the most basic marital questions, like 'Do I look fat in this?' or 'Is she prettier than I am?'

Even so, watching him teach our son how to cut his own nails made me fall in love with my husband all over again. I can only hope my boys grow up to be like him.

And that's a pretty good measure of a man, I think.

* * *

My husband is a fantastic guy, but all things considered, I think honeymoons are wasted on newlyweds. If you got married for all the right reasons, everything from washing the dishes to taking out the garbage together can be romantic in those early days. There's no good reason to blow a wad of cash on a fancy getaway.

I realized it was time to finally cash in on the honeymoon I missed the day I discovered my wedding ring and my engagement ring have together rubbed a permanent callous on the palm of my left hand. There's a metaphor in that rough spot of skin, something about the hard work that goes into a marriage.

It had been five years since our wedding and I'd lost track of the number of times I'd missed out on a full night of sleep, five years since I'd gone to bed without the expectation that someone might crawl uninvited into my bed or that I might give birth.

Well and truly ready for a break, to celebrate my 40th birthday my husband and I ditched the kids and went to Paris for the weekend.

From a practical standpoint, the easiest way to make economy seats more comfortable is to travel long distances for five years with toddlers. The first airplane seat I sat in without a child on my lap felt like a plush recliner, and I re-discovered that people watching in the transit lounge was a lot more entertaining since I could actually watch people other than the two little ones I'd brought with me.

I didn't even mind (very much) when the wind caught my dress as I departed the plane, blowing it up as high as my head. Having my underwear on display without my permission only served as a reminder of all the times my kids have inadvertently done the same.

And by the end of the weekend, after plenty of sleep and adult conversation, I found myself rushing back to the children I missed so much I could hardly remember why I needed a break in the first place.

* * *

Sure, there are days when I need some time away from my family, but most of the time, I'm overjoyed to have them around. I woke up one morning to find this note from my husband:

'Bomb threat in Dubai last night. No sleep so sleeping in and going to work at 8.30. Don't wake me. Thanks. ☺'

On the same day, my biggest news was that I'd won a really cool mobile phone on the radio because I'd been able to fake the best insincere laugh in response to a bad joke. That was the highlight of my entire week, in fact.

It was on that day that I began to realize just how difficult it must be for my husband. I sometimes give him a hard time when he comes home late from work and doesn't rush to spend time with the kids. But the folks at DreamWorks have done an excellent job making a point that most children will miss.

In the opening scenes of the last *Shrek* movie, *Forever After*, Fiona wishes that every day would be just like the one she and Shrek have shared that day, changing diapers, keeping the house in order and dealing with the general mayhem of having a family.

And it is.

Over and over again, Shrek's time is filled with noise and mess and annoying people. The DreamWorks people show in stark images what a lot of people don't know - that a lot of the time, fatherhood is a much bigger job than many dads let on, supporting a family and keeping everyone happy.

I like to think my husband and I understand each other, but in truth I don't always know what his life is like. Most days, he leaves for work between 7.30 and 8.00 in the morning. Though his work day officially ends at 4.30pm, he often stays behind to get all of his work done. It's nothing unusual for him to get home between 6.30 and 7.00 in the evening.

In contrast, by the grace of a benevolent boss, I work hours that allow me to take the kids to school at 8.00 in the morning and pick them up at 3.00 in the afternoon. One day last week, however, I was stuck in the office working one of those seemingly endless marathon days my husband works most of the time.

By the time I got home, I was exhausted. And while I really wanted to give the kids a squeeze and tell them how much I loved them, I also wanted to sit in a quiet room by myself even more. Instead, I got them bathed and ready for bed, poorly succeeding in keeping my foul mood in check.

Yes, being a mom is hard work, especially for those women who have another job in addition to being a parent (*all* mothers are working mothers - it's just a question of how many jobs you have).

At this very moment, as I write, my oldest son is bouncing around the lounge room still in his pajamas at 2.30 on a Saturday afternoon. My youngest is stretching across my notes trying to reach the pointy stick I've just taken away from him and they're watching the grossly politically incorrect 1953 version of Peter Pan.

But however hard my days may be, they're nothing compared to the sheer volume of hours my husband has worked in his effort to have us well cared for, the volume of hours he has to look forward to in the years to come, hours I deeply appreciate.

OK, maybe he does need a cave.

WIFING

One thing you should know about Abu Dhabi is that pretty much everyone who has kids has a nanny. While there's no doubt life is certainly easier when you've got someone to do your laundry and wash your floors, at least part of the reason so many moms hire help is that there are literally hundreds of women in Abu Dhabi who are looking for honest work.

The nanny I have at the moment is putting her three teenage boys through school in the Philippines on the wages we pay her. With no free schools in the Philippines, her boys would otherwise not be able to go to school at all. So yes, I *could* wash my own clothes and dishes, but I'd be taking the food right off of their table and what sort of woman would that make me?

It's also the fact that having a nanny is often easier than fighting for one of the few infant spots in the nursery schools. Who wouldn't prefer their newborn to have one-on-one attention than to being part of a class?

When my oldest son was born, I was still teaching high school, and the cheapest, most convenient option was to find a nanny to look after my baby while I was at work. And while she came from Sri Lanka, my first nanny was surprisingly very like my mother.

I had a sneaking suspicion about how things were going to pan out when I found myself arguing with her one morning. OK, it wasn't really an argument. She suggested I store the bread in the refrigerator and I said the refrigerator makes the bread go hard. She answered with one of those raised-eyebrow, tilt-of-the-head expressions only mothers can use to say everything they need to say without saying a word.

The bread stayed in the refrigerator.

All my suspicions were confirmed when I caught her diluting the dishwashing liquid with water and rinsing out used plastic Ziploc bags.

Like my mother from West Texas, my Sri Lankan nanny grew up believing that there's no reason to use full strength dish soap and you shouldn't simply throw away a perfectly good plastic bag when it can be reused. We were always very sensitive about the environment when we were growing up, recycling cans for cash and reusing everything we could. We called it 'being poor'.

And it's not just me. My friend Vanessa recalls the day she was leaving for work when her nanny asked her, in that innocuous way of mothers, 'Is that what you're wearing today?'

Vanessa turned around and went back upstairs to change.

The benefit of having hired my virtual mother was that my first nanny loved my children as much as she loves her own. For four years, she spoiled them rotten and sneaked them chocolate and cared for them in a way that no mere employee could. You just can't put a price on that.

According to the country's labor laws, most expatriates are only allowed to work in the UAE until the age of 60. When our first nanny reached that age, she had to return to Sri Lanka and I spent the next year and a half without any professional help.

By this time, I'd graduated from teaching to writing. The plan was that I would do my freelance writing work in the mornings while my children were at nursery school, and then spend the afternoons looking after the house while looking after the kids at the same time.

It was one of the hardest years of my life.

It seemed every morning brought some new emergency that kept me out of the house in the morning – bills to be paid, errands to be run, groceries to be bought. More often than I liked, my afternoons were spent trying to keep the kids entertained while I sat at the computer working, and those days generally ended in disaster.

One day I gave the kids muffins, hoping to buy myself another half hour to meet a deadline. By the time I emerged from my office, I discovered that the children had covered the entire house in an even layer of crumbs. I could not have had a bigger mess on my hands if I'd loaded the muffins into a shotgun and pulled the trigger.

Freelance writing eventually gave way to a permanent job with a weekly magazine, *Abu Dhabi Week*, and I've been there ever since. If you've been in Abu Dhabi, you might recognize parts of this book from my Motherload column which appears on the family page of the magazine.

After 15 childless years spent teaching, I finally have two children, a regular office job and no school holidays.

Now, there are around 60 weekdays of the year during which the kids are out of school, and that's not counting all those random days of illness I can't predict. Even if I cough up the expensive fees for a six-week summer camp, there are a lot days in between when I'm working and my kids are home.

When the magazine offered me a job, I tried to get by without a nanny, but after six months I gave up and decided to hire another nanny.

Which is a lot easier said than done.

In my search to replace our brilliant Sri Lankan nanny, I met a whole range of unsuitable candidates. Some potential employees had no sense of punctuality while others would wait for hours until *after* they were due to arrive to call and say they couldn't make it. Some simply disappeared never to return.

One was unable to take the children outside to play one afternoon because she said she 'couldn't find the door'. Another didn't feed my youngest for six hours because she 'couldn't find the rice' despite the mountain of other food in the kitchen.

The one after her didn't bother to change my son's diaper for six hours and the one after *her* assumed that my five year old would be able to sort himself out for snacks and lunch in the same period of time, even though I had left everything prepared.

Another potential candidate believed wiping my children's hands and faces with a wet wipe constituted a 'bath' while yet another assumed I wouldn't mind if she replaced the $20 note in my purse with a $10.

After a lot of looking – *a lot* – I finally found an experienced, friendly Filipina lady, and I count myself lucky to have her. All I can say is, whoever said being a mother was easy should try finding a subcontractor to do the job.

* * *

Though it's not as urgent as finding a good nanny, for a lot of reasons, it's hard to find a hairdresser in Abu Dhabi that won't make me cry. Too often stylists won't give me the cut I ask for, or they charge an obscene amount of money, or they assume that because I'm a certain age and nationality I absolutely must have a particular style.

I recently trusted a new hairdresser to cut the rangy mess that had grown halfway down my back into what I'd hoped would be a funky, tousled, alluring short style. The mistake I made (other than showing up responsibly on time and unfashionably in flip flops) was to mention that I only had an hour because my children were in the crèche.

Now, just because I'm overjoyed to be a mother doesn't mean I want to look like one. Unfortunately, thanks to my children, I'm now sporting the worst sort of style - Mom Hair, the type my own mother would describe as 'appropriate'.

The trouble with 'appropriate' is that, in the history of mankind, the captain of the football team has never swept up the nerdy girl in school and said, 'Hey baby, your hair is *so* suitable and conservative. You look almost exactly like my mom. Want to make out in the back seat of my car?'

In retrospect, I never should have mentioned the crèche. Instead, I should have told the stylist that my husband - um, I mean, my tattooed boyfriend who's the leader of a biker gang and wears a lot of leather - was waiting for me. On his Harley Fatboy. I might have gotten a better result.

It doesn't matter, though. No matter how bad my hair looks, my little boys still think I'm 'brootiful'.

* * *

My hair isn't the only feature to fall victim to my motherhood. I shouldn't complain about my stomach, I really shouldn't. I managed two pregnancies without any stretch marks or Caesarean scars. But while my stomach was never as flat as a pancake before I had kids, these days it's starting to look more and more like a bagel.

I knew it was time to take matters in hand when I went swimming with my family one weekend. A trio of snarky teenage girls on holiday from the UK was lounging beside my favorite pool in Abu Dhabi.

From my spot sitting on the edge of the water, it wasn't long before I realized that the 'hot guy' the teen girls were all gushing about was my husband who was splashing with our boys not far away.

Even worse, when I got out of the water, the three of them locked eyes on my midsection. Without tearing their gazes away from my stomach, the three little bitches started whispering amongst themselves.

In unison they shrieked with laughter and pointed *at my stomach*, and for the rest of the afternoon every time I walked by, they spoke just loudly enough for me to hear them laugh and describe my body as 'gross', 'disgusting' and simply 'ewwww!'

I was shamed into wearing my fat-tini for months – you know, the two piece variety of bathing suit with a full length top that tries to be a one piece for grandmothers.

Clearly it's time to make the most of my new nanny and start running again. Nasty girls notwithstanding, I don't expect washboard abs. It's just that it's been years since the birth of my last child and I'd be happy if people would stop asking if I'm pregnant.

Goals don't get more realistic than that.

* * *

Of course, if I was a cave lady, I wouldn't have to worry about my weight – I'd spend enough time performing hard manual labor that it would all come off of its own accord – but then, times have changed.

A hundred years ago, the thought of buying food for a newborn baby never crossed anyone's mind. Admittedly, plenty of babies died back then because there was no infant formula to fill the gap when a mother wasn't able to produce enough breast milk.

There are plenty of good reasons for not breastfeeding that have to do with the health and sanity of both mother and baby. What's completely ridiculous is the argument against breastfeeding in public.

Thanks to its large Muslim population, Abu Dhabi is a pretty conservative town, and no mother in her right mind would consider feeding her baby in such a way that her body would be inappropriately exposed.

Even so, a lot of moms in this city (and around the world) feel like they have to hide out to give their newborns the most nutritious substance babies can ingest for fear of anyone knowing what they're doing.

Can I be the one to clarify that there is nothing alluring about breastfeeding? When, in the history of babies, has a man looked at a woman feeding her tiny infant and said, 'Hey, you sexy thing, is that some other dude's kid? Let's get it on!'

Even worse are the people who say ridiculous things like, 'I don't like to see a woman breastfeeding. I just never know where to look.'

Seriously? You don't know where to *look*?

Yeah, maybe if she was breastfeeding while at the same time pole dancing. I mean, country singer Dolly Pardon is famous the world over for her curves, and even *she* gives us other things to look at besides those two bouncy glands that my boys call my 'boots'.

Once and for all - moms, don't be ashamed to feed your babies with your breast milk because that's what 'boots' are for. And the rest of you, feel free to look *anywhere else* by turning your head.

Because that's what necks are for.

* * *

Breastfeeding is nothing to worry about, but planning for a day out with two little kids? Now *that's* serious.

When I really want to push some buttons, I know I can drive my husband crazy by repeating back to him whatever he's just said in a mocking version of his Australian accent. When he's trying to make the point that I'm overreacting and incompetent, he loves to tell me what a 'big deal' I'm making of something he says is easy.

It doesn't happen often, but every now and then, he lives to rue those words.

Like the day we went to Dubai shortly after my youngest son was born. I'd won a voucher to go painting at a drop-in art studio and, rather than leave the children at home with the nanny, my husband magnanimously offered to take them to the enormous Mall of the Emirates while I spent three much needed hours by myself in the studio two blocks away.

Now, the little one was just weeks old and the older one was not quite two years old, so I suggested my husband strap the baby onto his chest with our handy baby belly-pack carrier and push the big one in the massive pram that has a pouch underneath large enough to carry an afternoon's worth of equipment for two little kids.

Foolishly, my husband spoke the fatal words: 'For God's sake, Laura – what's the big deal? They're just two kids. You act like it's all so difficult.'

Without another word, I dropped him off at the mall with the kids and went to enjoy my afternoon.

While I drank coffee and created horrible art, my husband spent perhaps the worst afternoon of his life. He'd envisioned strolling through the mall with the baby in the pram and the toddler walking serenely by his side. He'd probably thought they would both stand quietly by while he did a bit of browsing.

Instead, the moment my husband got them both inside the mall, the toddler took off like a shot into the heavy weekend crowds and the baby started crying.

Instead of wandering serenely around the shops, he spent his afternoon carrying a squirming, crying newborn in one hand - trying not to drop him - and pushing our gigantic pram with the other, only barely keeping up with the toddler he didn't have a spare hand to corral.

When I called him two and a half hours later to tell him I was finished and did he want me to go ahead and come pick him up early, he was practically in tears.

See? No big deal.

* * *

While I might be pretty good at managing two kids at the mall (sort of), it turns out what I'm not so good at is dodging the authorities. Last week, it finally happened - I rolled the dice one time too many and got busted.

It's true that it's a lot easier to find parking in Abu Dhabi these days thanks to the municipality's new system of paid parking, but there's no denying it's still a pain in the backside. I now spend at least as much time hunting for coins to pay for my parking as I once did looking for a space. I'm forever without those essential coins when I need them.

I discovered several weeks ago, however, that you only have to pay for parking if there's someone to issue you a ticket when you *don't* pay. I've ducked into many a shop to conduct five quick minutes of business without paying for my blue and white space.

Last week, however, this cavalier attitude towards the parking authorities finally caught up with me. I would have paid for a space, but there were none left at 9pm outside a convenient grocery store. Given no other reasonable choice, I parked in a yellow zone and came out laden with shopping bags to find I'd been slugged with a fine for over $100.

Don't tell my husband.

So when I screeched into the parking lot of the bank yesterday, moments before closing, I was too scared to risk parking without a ticket in my windshield. Now, some spaces cost two dirham coins but the premium spots cost three. After a quick search, I discovered I had exactly two dirhams in my possession.

I dashed to the machine hoping against hope that the fee was only two coins but of course I was wrong and the only spaces available to me cost *three* dirhams. Watching me dig through my bag in frantic despair, a kind stranger took pity on me and gave me the third coin I needed. I jammed the coins into the machine and grabbed my ticket.

Of course, as I went to put the ticket into my car window, catastrophe struck. A gust of wind snatched the tiny scrap of paper from my fingers and swept it in a spiral five stories into the air. I spent the next five minutes literally running in circles and jumping up and down trying to catch the precious white square.

It finally landed on the ground and after a quick scrabble in the parking lot, I had it in my grip again. The same kind stranger who'd given me the third coin slowed as he walked by to tell me I looked like the funny British nincompoop Mr. Bean. Just in case I'd missed it.

I ran into the bank just in time to see the guard beginning to close the security gate. Again, I had to run for it – by this stage I was fully prepared to slide on my backside across the linoleum like a baseball player coming into home base or Indiana Jones escaping peril.

The good news is that I avoided a fine, I got to the teller after all and I now have a roll of 40 shiny dirham coins, plus a firm vow to collect all random coins that come my way. The bad news is that everyone who uses my bank thinks I'm an idiot.

Fair enough.

* * *

As you can see, I'm a pretty down-to-earth kind of gal. I don't mind getting sweaty in the gym, I'll make a fool of myself on the radio if there's a good prize on the line and I've been seen in public once or twice with a ponytail and no make-up on. Even so, I'd always thought I was a reasonably dignified person.

Until I had kids.

Take, for example, the simple act of shopping for clothes. There was once a time I could go swishing around the shops, browsing here, trying on cute outfits there. Now when I shop, I invariably have my children with me. When they start playing hide and seek, I can only steer them out of the couture towards the sale racks and hope for the best.

I remember trying to shop for bras once when my little one had just learned to walk. I was sure he'd be able to sit quietly on the floor while I determined whether or not I'd gone up a size. But the moment I was stripped to the waist, he discovered there was just enough space at the bottom of the change room door for him to wiggle under, through the store and into the mall at large.

Thankfully a clerk kept him from making his great escape, saving me the humiliation of running into the wide corridor of the crowded shopping mall wearing nothing but a grimace – but it was a close call.

And that was shopping with just *one* kid in tow. Plenty of ladies in this city have seen me in all my glory thanks to the number of times I've had to try on clothes with the door to my change room purposefully open so that I can keep an eye on my pair of hooligans.

Can I tell you how hard it is getting clothes that may or may not fit on and off with just one hand, using the other to keep a certain inquisitive toddler from going on a tour of change rooms? Almost as hard as it is to hang wet clothes on the line with a baby on my hip.

That I can still look all of you in the eye is nothing short of amazing.

* * *

In addition to all the moments I've been embarrassed on account of my children, for a lot of reasons, having kids can also be hazardous to your health.

For starters, we sort of have kids to blame for the sudden rise of worldwide fatness. After years of advances in medicine, for the first time in centuries the life expectancy of many people on Earth is shorter today than in the past because of obesity-related diseases. Hundreds of years of medical science brought to its knees by gravy.

Why? Because in the olden days, most mothers stayed home to shop and cook, but these days, we moms are expected to work a full-time job and bring home a full-time salary, or else we're considered to be lazy. If we hire a nanny to help us out, we're lazy because 'the nanny does everything' and if we gain weight as a result of childbearing, we're accused of letting ourselves go and being lazy.

And it's not just the fatness.

My oldest son nearly gave me a stroke at church one Palm Sunday. It wasn't that he was brandishing a certain relic of our Lord like it was Zorro's sword – I don't expect a five year old to understand the significance of an object that actually looks a lot like a rapier when you hold it upside down.

No, the vein in my forehead started throbbing when he refused to hand the palm cross to me and then *ran away* from me and *into the aisle* where I had to *chase* him. In front of the entire congregation.

My boys have coughed directly into my mouth often, and I've spent a combined total of weeks of my life breathing contaminated air on the planes we've ridden around the globe. In our rush to get it all done, too often we moms rely on fast food to fill the gap and we narrowly avoid falling down dead of stress-related afflictions.

But then my little son stops amid the flurry, looks up at me for no reason at all and says, 'I love you, Mommy' and suddenly my heart rate returns to normal and I'm reminded why people with loving families generally live longer than bitter single people who die alone.

Yeah, raising kids is one giant scurry, but I guess like dirt and snot and grass stains on pants, it all comes out in the wash.

* * *

What doesn't come out in the wash is wrinkles. Or gray hair. Or cellulite. And like a lot of women, I spend a lot of time disappointed with my appearance.

A few years ago, however, when I was pregnant and radiant, the hormones simmering away in my belly had done such a number on my self-esteem that most mornings I thought I was absolutely beautiful.

Needing to renew my passport, I washed my hair, put on some lip gloss and glided down the street to my neighborhood photo shop one afternoon to get my picture taken, confident the photographer would find me gorgeous.

By the time the new passport was ready, my hormone level had evened out, and the celluloid revealed what the mirror had not. While I might have been a radiant pregnant mother, I was also wearing eight months of baby fat, and my face was as wide as a barn door.

The Fat Face Photo was the ID picture I used to startle gate agents at airports around the world until my passport was stolen in Malaysia last Christmas. Needing emergency passports from two different embassies just to leave the country, we all had to get new passport photos immediately.

I was not at all surprised when this set of photos came back within the hour. I'd sweated off what little make-up I'd been wearing in the tropical heat, my frazzled ponytail was starting to fly away in bits and I had bags under my eyes. In short, I looked like...

Well, like I'd just gotten robbed in Malaysia.

When I finally got my permanent passport months later, I discovered that my renewed residence visa bore the pregnant photo while the main page showed my stressed out Malaysian photo. I've now captured the worse of my mothering looks from conception through the present day, preserved in my most valuable document until 2020. Fantastic.

I ought to *really* shock the gate agents with this one.

* * *

It's also pretty shocking how bad I am with my phone. When it comes to inventions, the iPhone is a really great one. When I convinced my husband that I absolutely needed one for work, I had no idea just how much I'd come to depend on the sleek little miracle of technology.

Of course it's my phone and email and internet, but it's also the alarm clock that wakes me up at 5.30am to go running, it's the electronic notepad I use to write on-the-spot reviews and interviews and it's the music player that keeps me motivated in the gym.

If you've been keeping track, however, the very last thing I need is something else to distract me. I can't count the number of times I've stepped off a curb while trying to respond to a text and nearly fallen flat on my face, or bumped into walls trying to find exactly the song I want.

And I don't even know how to do applications. Let me figure *that* out and someone is likely to take my children away from me for their own safety.

It's not like I'm doing silly things like texting while I'm driving, but I was so distracted answering an important email when I went to pick up my son from nursery the other day that I was half way to the car before it registered with me what my littlest one had been trying to tell me with increasing frenzy.

I'd picked up the wrong backpack and was ready to take home some other kid's bag. Thankfully my three year old was paying more attention than I was.

I mean, I've accepted that my five year old is more capable of keeping track of his school timetable than I am. But when I need my three year old to stop me from stealing from his classmates, well, something needs to be done.

It's a sad state of affairs, but if I don't find a way to just set down the phone and walk away, I'm almost certain that it's going to be the end of me. I'll step into traffic or concuss myself or accidentally end my days by electrocution, and I can just see the coroner's report now – death by iPhone.

* * *

If driving – or, for me, walking – down the roads of Abu Dhabi is dangerous, I should confess that one thing we all love about living in Abu Dhabi is the virtual absence of crime. While the nearest town down the road, Dubai, has had its fair share of mafia robberies and high profile assassinations, Abu Dhabi remains one of the safest cities in the world.

This town is so safe, in fact, that it is commonplace for people to leave their cars unlocked, many times with the keys in the ignition and engine running, while they go inside a building for sometimes surprising lengths of time.

One scorching June afternoon shortly after I first met the guy I'd end up marrying, I popped into Subway for some lunch. It was too hot to turn off the car, so I left the engine running, even though it was my new boyfriend's car, the same boyfriend who would become my husband in a few months' time.

When I ducked back into the driver's seat, sandwiches in hand, I noticed for the first time a bottle of cologne I didn't know my then-boyfriend liked, a shirt on the floor I'd never seen him wear, all kinds of evidence of a life I didn't know he had.

It wasn't until I tried to put the key into the ignition and it didn't fit that I realized I was sitting in the wrong car. I found the owner of the Mitsubishi Outlander identical to mine (which was parked three spaces down) standing patiently in the doorway of the shop *he'd* popped into, waiting to see how long it would take me to discover my mistake.

Surprised as I was that day, it was nothing compared to what happened a year later to that same boyfriend – now my husband – outside a popular grocery store in the city one night. He'd parked properly, turned off and locked his car to go inside to shop, but when he returned, he found that someone in a giant Land Cruiser had parked behind him, blocking him in.

Though most people will leave their mobile phone number in their windshield in just such cases, my husband couldn't find a number, and while he didn't want to call the police, he also had places to be.

After waiting around for several minutes, it seemed logical to him that since the engine of the Land Cruiser was running, it would be the work of just a moment for him to hop into the errant car and back it up a few feet. He was almost certain the driver wouldn't mind.

He'd just dodged a bevy of cars on the busy road to slide into the driver's seat when a strange squawk from the darkened interior startled him. He almost fell out of the car and into oncoming traffic when he finally noticed what was perched on the centre console.

There sat a giant, majestic hunting falcon, complete with feathered hood and in no mood to make friends with strangers. The good-humored owner came running up just in time to see my husband recovering from his near coronary.

Which just goes to prove that while Abu Dhabi may be safe, it's not for the faint of heart.

THE SKINNY

Summer 2009

It's been just over two years since the birth of my youngest child and I'm convinced, in my inexpert opinion, that there is something wrong with me. I know that none of my writing courses in graduate school covered anything to do with endocrinology or hormone irregularities, but there *has* to be an explanation for what's going on with my body these days.

When my second son turned ten months old just over a year ago, I'd been either pregnant or breastfeeding or pregnant *and* breastfeeding for thirty months in a row, and I hadn't had even one decent night's sleep in almost three years.

Convinced that a complete switch to solids would finally fill up my little Gemini long enough that he would no longer make demands of my glands in the middle of *every single* night of his life, I cut him off and reclaimed my body.

From that the time until just a few months ago, things went from bad to worse. My punishment for ripping my infant son too soon from my weary bosoms, it seems, has been a slow but certain deterioration of my own body image, complete with belly fat, mood swings, hard core fatigue and moments of black rage punctuated with afternoons spent weighing the potential pros and cons of a life of alcoholism.

The good news is that it turns out I lack the commitment to become a truly dedicated alcoholic; the bad news is that if there's nothing biologically amiss, I'll be forced to accept that I'm just a bitch.

What else can explain those months I spent screaming at other motorists, suddenly shaking with rage at the sort of bad driver I've encountered every day since I moved to this town, drivers who should no longer be able to surprise me?

What else can justify the resentment I felt equally towards everyone from my innocent husband to the guys who blew up the World Trade Center to the sacker at the grocery store who put the bag of potatoes on top of the bag of potato chips?

'In the name of all things holy!' I remember shrieking at the poor guy. 'Heavy things go on the bottom *and light things go on top!!!*'

I've never used the F word more in my life.

Even worse, all the caloric benefit I'd gained from breastfeeding was lost. Since breastfeeding burns around 500 calories a day, my baby weight practically dropped off – I got down to 57kg, about 125lbs. That's my college, skinny, hot girl weight, five pounds less than I'd been when I inexplicably bagged my husband in the first place.

Once those 500 calories a day returned to my plate, however, the pounds started creeping back on. By the end of last year's hellishly hot summer, I was back up to my wedding weight and still climbing.

In an effort to keep the weight at bay, I started training for my third marathon. Six weeks into training, however, I fell over a tricycle and the injury I'd sustained in my left knee running the first two marathons was exacerbated to the point that I had to give up running altogether.

The minute I quit training, what had been a slow decline in fitness and mental acuity snowballed into an avalanche of cellulite and ill will towards all mankind.

My mood reached its lowest point about nine months ago when I spent many long afternoons lying on the couch watching the children play and wondering exactly what the hell the point was supposed to be. I remember one day watching my son from across the room. He had a bit of a cold and his nose was running freely.

'When the snot gets to his mouth, I'll get up and wipe it,' I consciously thought to myself.

I can see now that I was showing classic symptoms of depression, but when you're neck deep in trees, it doesn't always look like a forest.

The final straw broke a couple of weeks later on our yearly trip to Australia, that horrific journey of flying standby and staying in Hell's Rental Cottage. When we finally arrived at the shack in Cudgee, my body protested in every way it knew how – I had a migraine that left me throwing up every thirty minutes for a whole day and a spontaneous menstrual cycle.

'You need to get this shit sorted out,' my uterus was trying to tell me, 'or I'll let you bleed to death right here in the Australian outback.'

When I got home a couple of weeks later, I went to three different doctors hoping for an explanation. For all that's great about living in Abu Dhabi, reliable healthcare isn't one of them – it's hit and miss at best. (At least it was while I was there.)

Still, it had been ten months of gaining weight, feeling tired and hating everyone. Throw in a phantom period and a migraine, and I felt I was being reasonable when I concluded that something was really wrong.

The first doctor I went to attributed the entire affair to stress caused by jetlag, and after five minutes sent me on my way with a recommendation to take Vitamin C.

Dr Number Two had the decency to at least round up the usual suspects. He performed an extensive pap smear, a pelvic examination and even an ultrasound. At least I think he was acting out of decency. He was the only male gynecologist at the hospital. The clerk charged with booking appointments couldn't believe I was actually willing to see him.

'But madam,' the bewildered clerk said when I called to make the appointment, 'he is a *male* doctor.'

'Is he a qualified gynecologist?' I asked.

'Yes, but he is a *male* doctor.'

'But he's a gynecologist, right?'

'Yes?' *And your point would be?* she seemed to be suggesting.

'Then I'll see him. When is his earliest appointment?'

'Oh, madam. He has no appointments. Come any time.'

After in depth analysis, Dr Number Two came to the inexplicable conclusion that, since my tests were all normal, my symptoms might be caused by Irritable Bowel Syndrome. How can I trust a gynecologist who can't tell my coochie from a hole in my ass?

As a last resort, I went to a very swank private clinic in a very swank suburb of Dubai. Dr Number Three, a Bulgarian woman, performed all the same tests that I'd told her Dr Number Two had found to be normal plus one blood test. Her advice, which came with a hefty bill for all those tests, was this: 'Take evening primrose oil. It's an herbal supplement, but if you think it will work, then it will.'

Which is just a fancy way of saying that it's all in my head. I couldn't make her understand that it's not in my head. It's mostly in my butt and my thighs and my white-knuckled, clenched fists.

Ironically, the day of the untimely Australian period seemed to be a double-edged turning point. Since that time, my mood seems better but I'm only getting fatter and fatter. I've gotten so fat, in fact, that my husband has finally noticed.

Now, you can get a lot past my husband. He doesn't notice little things like whether or not the floor is clean or how many nights in a row the kids have eaten chicken nuggets for dinner, but when he came home from work a month ago, I was finally fat enough to get his attention.

He made some innocuous comment about the chips and dip I'd been eating without pausing to breathe as I cooked dinner - to which I responded that I'd been trying to lose weight. Up to that point, my efforts had been half hearted at best, so my husband (who is scathingly honest) wanted to know exactly *what* I had been doing to lose weight.

Thus launched what will go down in the annals of our marriage as The Fat Fight. He wanted to know why I wasn't toned anymore like I was when we met. And while I didn't say it out loud, I wanted to grab a double fistful of his love handles and ask him where - if my cooking was so bad - had all of *this* come from.

The argument ended when he poked a roll of my hip fat bulging over the waistband of my shorts and I started crying.

Since then, he's begged my forgiveness. I reminded him that a man with an expensive life insurance policy and a legally binding will shouldn't criticize the size of the woman who cooks his food.

I've also made a really concerted effort to lose weight. I've been running and lifting weights and I've been paying real attention to my diet. I haven't had McDonalds, I've consumed mountains of raw vegetables in lieu of real food and I've eaten oatmeal while my family eats bacon and pancakes. I'm hoping that if they're all fat, I might look thinner by comparison. The result? So far, I've lost...

...exactly nothing. Not even one single, solitary ounce.

In fact, I'm actually fatter now than I was when I began this regime. Clothes that I wore two months ago are now so tight that I can't even get them on. In the same length of time, however, my contrite husband has managed to 'accidentally' lose 20 pounds playing nine holes of golf once a week, pancakes and bacon notwithstanding.

The bastard.

Experts on MSN's many fitness web pages tell me that the only way I can have a flat stomach at my age is to eat nothing but fish, broccoli and water. I can't have sweets, caffeine, alcohol or fried foods. Even fruit is full of natural sugar, they say. I say, what's the point of living in a world without bacon and red meat and beer?

A life without bacon couldn't possibly end well. I can just hear the hostage negotiators now: 'See that homicidal maniac crouched in the corner over there? The one who didn't eat her bacon? Yes, that one with the shotgun? Damn, she's got good abs.'

So I made an appointment with a fourth doctor. I was interested to see how this went. When I told her that I thought my thyroid might be to blame, she suggested over the phone that I see a dietician.

Trying to make clear to this woman that something needed to happen and soon, I wrote her a lengthy email. There I sat at my computer at nearly 3.00 in the morning, unable to sleep. My bathrobe was getting tight and little wonder. I was up to 68kg – almost 150lbs – which is what I weighed when I was pregnant.

Even worse, I knew that the next morning when my husband went to work, I'd be dead dog tired and my poor children would have to spend the day listening to their mommy screaming along with trailer park rap by Limp Bizkit.

I needed to make Dr Number Four understand that I couldn't go back. The fatness was only one symptom – I couldn't go back to being the sad, angry, tired, crazy bitch I'd been nine months before. I couldn't go back to wishing that Child Protective Services had an afternoon drop-off service.

Above all else, I couldn't have another Fat Fight. I was standing on the precipice, staring into the chasm of insanity. Considering the mood I was teetering on the brink of, if my husband were to poke my fat, I probably would have stabbed him in the neck with a meat fork. And knowing my luck, I'd end up with the only anorexic cellmate on D Block.

'If you're going to be *my* prison bitch,' I could just hear her saying, 'you're going to need to do a few sit-ups. The elastic waistband of that orange jumpsuit isn't doing you any favors.'

So I made another drive to Dubai, desperate to find a doctor who wouldn't confuse my digestive tract with my reproductive system.

After a long, difficult drive during which I got so lost that I finally paid a taxi driver to guide me to the doctor's office while my youngest son yanked the portable DVD player into two pieces in the back seat, I was in a right black mood.

A lengthy wait later and it was finally time to see the doctor. I was sure she would be reasonable – she was a cute, elfish-looking woman from Australia, after all. She began with a detailed questionnaire that made me feel like I was in the hands of a true professional.

Until the last question.

'Do you smoke?' she asked. I was confident this was one question I would get points for answering correctly.

'No, I never have.'

'Are you sure?' The skepticism was clear on her face. She did not believe me.

'Yes, I'm sure.'

'Not at all? Not even on the weekends? Because smoking can cause weight gain and if you're not honest with these questions I can't help you.' Again, nothing but disdain on her sneering little pixie face.

What I wanted to say was this: Do you actually think I would take the time to drive over an hour in the company of a two year old, get lost and pay you almost $300 to *lie* to you? Do you honestly believe that I'm *that* brand of insane? Do you understand that there are hundreds of empty square miles between here and Abu Dhabi, any one of which would be the perfect spot for me to bury your dead body if I finally snap right this minute and kill you?

'No, I *really don't* smoke,' I said calmly, a nerve under my right eye starting to twitch.

'Because I can smell smoke on you.'

Of all the things I have to admit to having done in my life, one thing I've *never* done was drugs or smoke. It was just about more than I could take. For all the money I'd spent, for all the visits to all the doctors, this one wasn't hearing me any more than any of the rest of them had.

When she went on to recommend I see her clinic's dietician – which would cost over $200 – I stopped listening. I was on my own. Again.

* * *

Summer 2011

I wrote the first part of this chapter about two years ago and you'll be relieved to know, I'm sure, that since that time, things have taken a turn for the better and I'm finally (mostly) skinny again.

It started with a fitness program I took on nearly six months ago, a New Year's resolution that managed to stick for once. Like others I've embarked upon in the course of my adulthood, this program involved lots of exercise and healthy eating but it was several weeks before I saw any real results.

Having given my bad knee several months to heal, I started running with my neighbor and the weight finally started coming off.

The truth, though, is that the running may have been just a coincidence. The combined total of all the calories I burn running four kilometers a day three times a week is less than 1500 calories, and to lose a pound, I need to create a calorie deficit of 3500. To lose *one* pound.

I've managed to create that very deficit, though, to the tune of 12kg so far. That's over 26lbs. Where did the other 2000 calories a week come from?

Easy – eating less. A *lot* less. Apparently, you really *can* live without bacon.

It took me awhile to realize how much emotional eating I'd been doing. All those long months of screaming and laying on the couch in abject despair, I was eating pretty much everything in sight. I ate when I was stressed, bored, worried, celebrating, working, driving, resting, watching TV and socializing.

Without my giving it a conscious thought, food became my mother, my best friend and my fling on the side. That's a lot to ask of a Big Mac, but if you can believe it, a Big Mac is burger enough to rise to the challenge. Fritos Scoops with salsa washed down with gin and tonic are pretty reliable too.

Since nobody else can tell me what's wrong with me, I've been forced to diagnose myself with a disorder of my own invention, one I'm calling *I'm Not Just A Bitch*, (INJAB for short).

> Appendix E: Symptoms of INJAB, or
> I May Be a Bitch but I'm Not *Just* a Bitch –
> There *Really Is* Something Wrong with Me

- Fatigue, especially at the end of the day, that has little or no connection to how the kids sleep – and I mean bone weary, as in can't-get-up-off-the-couch-and-can't-think-of-a-reason-why-I'd-ever-want-to, please-kill-me-now tired

- Trouble sleeping through the night, occasionally waking up in the teensy hours of the morning unable to return to sleep, sometimes for over an hour, sometimes for the rest of the night

- Foul moods and black rages, lack of patience and the tendency to scream at everyone from my children to random ayatollahs in the news

- Depression punctuated by a feeling of negativity and hopelessness that generally *isn't* cured by copious amounts of gin combined with tonic

- Tendency to start crying in only moderately emotional situations – bursting into tears at anything from a disturbing headline to a TV commercial about puppies

- All kinds of typical hormonal misery surrounding That Special Time of the Month like irregular periods, migraine headaches, pimples, cramps, constipation and bloating

- The reintroduction of the really disturbing facial tic I first saw when I was in high school and could least afford that extra bit of weirdness – it's a bizarre flick of one cranial nerve that runs through my forehead that makes it look like I'm trying to send a secret signal to whoever is around me (12 shots of Botox seem to have wrestled it to a standstill – for the moment anyway)

- Weight gain from emotional eating

- General, garden variety stuff that may or may not be related like being clumsy and forgetful – but I'm willing to accept that those might just be me

Appendix F: Stuff That Helps (A Little)

- Drinking plenty of water and eating right (while at the same time thinking that there's practically no point in eating well when junk food is my most faithful friend)

- Limiting caffeine and alcohol (even though coffee and gin sometimes seem like more basic requirements to sustain life than oxygen)

- Getting enough sleep (ha! Cruel joke, that one)

- Not having too much stress to deal with (ha! Like I can control *that* sort of nonsense)

- Exercising regularly (but who can get up off the couch, much less lift weights?)

* * *

So you can imagine how eager I was to find an answer. While I still don't know the cause, I do finally have a solution.

About two years ago, I was visiting my good friend Susie in Boston - when I told her about my INJAB, she said she'd been taking something called Vitex to regulate her hormones. It's an herbal supplement, she told me, the extract of the fruit of the chasteberry bush.

Supposedly, monks once ate chasteberries to help control their libidinous urges. I figured it couldn't hurt to try.

Whatever it may have done for the monks, the Vitex changed my life. After three days of taking the pills, it was like all the angry glitter had finally started to settle to the bottom of the furious little snow globe of my mind.

For the first time in ages, I was happy and patient. I wasn't dog tired by the end of the day and the world in general looked like a pretty good spot to hang out for awhile.

After a few weeks, though, I stopped taking the Vitex. I thought it was responsible for the weeks of sleepless nights I'd spent scratching myself. By the time I discovered that the torturous itching had been caused not by the Vitex but instead by the bedbugs we'd accidentally brought home from a hotel down the street from Disneyland, I was almost out of pills.

Then six months ago, in conjunction with the Enough Already with the Fatness New Year's Resolution, I decided to give the Vitex another try. Since I haven't been able to find it in Abu Dhabi, I stocked up in Australia and started my fitness program.

At first, the Vitex only gave me the energy and give-a-damn I needed to exercise again for the first time in months, but within a few weeks it had managed to wrestle my hormones (or whatever it is) under control again.

These days I'm able to eat only when I'm hungry, sometimes not even then. OK, I probably still spend way more time obsessing about food than is healthy, but I reckon it's better to think about food than to eat it.

Naked in the Driveway

The only problem now is that I live in constant fear that someday the Vitex will stop working. As it is, the day before my period starts, I grow cloven hooves and horns from my head. If my husband ever leaves me, it will be on one of those days.

I'm only glad that I've been able to identify that I have a problem at all.

There are women I know who suffer from hormonal imbalance from the first day of their first period and it never goes away. The rage and depression are such a part of their biological systems that they don't realize there's a problem that they can fix – and neither does anyone else around them.

These poor gals go their whole lives thinking everything in the world sucks and whenever they're in the room, all their friends and family can think only one thing: 'Man, she is *such* a *bitch!*'

According to the tests I've had, there's nothing wrong with my thyroid or my hormone levels, I don't have endometriosis or any tumors and I'm not pregnant. I do know that I had similar symptoms when I was in high school which makes me think there's some sort of connection with my hormones. I assume all my symptoms are related, but I don't have conclusive evidence that they are or aren't.

All I know is that I can't be the only woman in the world suffering from INJAB. I'd like to have a back-up in case the Vitex ever fails me, so if you find a medical diagnosis more professional than mine, let me know. I'll either be holed up in a bell tower or the only woman on my cell block doing Pilates.

MOTHERLOAD

As much as I'm all for the equality of the sexes, there's no denying that there are certain areas in which women excel and certain things that men do better.

Women, for instance, are more likely to know the difference between periwinkle and lavender while men, in the main, are better at parallel parking.

In a remarkable show of faith, the directors of my son's nursery school have actually reconfigured the parking scheme in front of the school in such a way that we can only parallel park, which I personally think is a lot to ask of a bunch of harried mothers with children younger than four.

And while I know that plenty of girls are great at problem solving, I have to wonder if it wasn't the Y chromosome that was responsible for my oldest son's recent experiment.

When I caught him putting a button in his mouth one day, I told him to spit it out with the baleful threat that if he put the button in his mouth, he would surely choke and die.

Several weeks later, he found himself in class doing a school project that involved gluing buttons onto a cup. Remembering my menacing warning, he applied the scientific method to see if I was actually right or not.

Determining – I can only assume – that a button is smaller than a chicken nugget, he first formulated the theory that he would *not* actually die if he swallowed a button. To test his theory, he conducted at least one experiment and he came to a reasonable conclusion which he published by proclamation in the car on the way home.

'Because Mommy, I ate a button.' (Most of his sentences start with 'because' – it's his response to the question he's sure has been burning, unspoken, in my mind.)

When I asked if he'd eaten the button in response to peer pressure or to humor his friends – all of whom would be enormously amused by button eating, I'm certain – his response was no.

'But Mommy, I didn't die.'

He applied the same theory a week later and came to the conclusion that, while eating a button wouldn't kill him, it was the button that was responsible for his bout of the flu and that I *should* have told him eating buttons would make him sick. His teacher told him putting things in his mouth would make him sick and she, apparently, knows everything.

Now doesn't that sound like a boy thing?

* * *

Another great thing about having boys is the brotherly love. When I see my oldest take his little brother by the hand or hug him, I feel a tug in my throat and a tear in my eye. Watching them fight, however, makes me want to reach for the gin.

For a few short months, my oldest took untold pleasure in tormenting his toddling brother, tipping him over or taking his toy, but in that resilient character of human nature, my baby learned fast when to put up his dukes and fight the injustice.

These days, the boys are fairly evenly matched, 20 month age gap between them notwithstanding. My youngest will sometimes run. He's learned, though, that more often than not, it's best to stop, hunker down and make like a stone in the road, causing his brother to trip over him and go flying. That *has* to be very satisfying. If that doesn't work, raw fisticuffs usually do.

In response, the oldest has perfected the art of face clawing. More than once, my little one has walked away from a fight between them looking like he just got glassed in a pub brawl.

Sick of the fighting, I finally took a lesson from my good friends in Hollywood, one I picked up flipping TV channels late one night. Towards the end of *X-Men Origins*, Wolverine and his brother face a mutual enemy who can move anywhere in the blink of an eye. The siblings only defeat him by joining forces and standing with their backs to each other to fight the foe from two sides at the same time.

Now when I see my boys locked in combat, I make them stop and I ask, 'How do you fight with your brother?' to which they rush to stand Wolverine-style back to back. I hope someday they'll catch on to the whole 'you and me against the world' lesson I'm trying to teach.

Until then, at least they can't leave lasting marks when all they can do is bump backsides.

* * *

You'd think with my two little ruffians beating the crap out of each other I'd have my hands full, and I do. So it was with grudging goodwill that I took in the bedraggled kitten I found near the traffic whizzing along one of the busiest roads in town. Abu Dhabi is literally crawling with hundreds of feral cats that live on whatever they can find in the garbage bins, so everyone calls them bin cats.

Most bin cats, though skinny and humorless, are a tough breed. With never a really cold day to contend with and plenty of free food in the bins, they manage pretty well. Still, a lot of people pity them and sooner or later almost everyone ends up adopting one of these filthy, scrawny felines off the street.

The little kitten I found sitting smack in the middle of the side street was undoubtedly the most pitiable bin cat I'd seen in all my years living in Abu Dhabi.

Sure, she was tiny and bony, but even worse, one eyeball was missing altogether and the other was half blinded with some sort of post-viral gunk. As soon as I approached her, she ran away, bumping into a parked car on the way. I had no choice but to bring her in.

Partial blindness notwithstanding, it took me four hours, two nursery school teaching assistants, a borrowed towel, a turkey sandwich and the help of six Pakistani landscapers to catch this tiny, three month old spitfire.

Annoyed though I was at being guilted into adoption, I had to respect her survival instinct. I'd dodged the bin cat bullet for seven years, after all, so with a deep sigh, I bundled her off to the vet, naming her BeBe in honor of Bright Beginnings, the nursery outside of which I found her.

I'd hoped to simply do my civic duty and pay to have them put her down (charity indeed at $75) but the scrawny little beast insisted on being the picture of health, her damaged eyes her only malady. Over $100 later, she's now been de-sexed, vaccinated and treated as well as the vet can manage.

In return for my kindness, BeBe's gratitude for the first three months in our house consisted of biting the children and sulking under the bed. Fair enough – she'd survived her entire precarious life thanks to her savvy wariness.

After we returned from our first holiday away, she deigned to sit in the room with us. The next holiday saw her suffering us to pet her, but not for longer than five seconds at a time.

These days, she's mellowed into a reasonable animal. She will tolerate no kind of rubbish from the kids and will even chase them back to their beds if they get up after lights out at night, but she doesn't scratch the furniture or shed her fur or try to eat my food. She doesn't insist I pet her for hours on end. In fact, she's happy to follow me from room to room and sleep on the end of my bed at night.

It's taken her three years to learn how to purr, but now she finally sits in my lap in the evenings, buzzing away in contentment. And every time I hear her thunk into the wall, I'm glad all over that I rescued her from the street.

* * *

I'm sort of amazed my husband let me keep the cat, but as soon as she learned to rub up against his legs and lie beside him in bed, he caved and has accepted her as part of the family, funky eye and all.

Though he'd have you believe that he's not as much of a softie as I am (although in truth I think he's just as bad), I can say with certainty that he's generally a pretty responsible guy. His job, after all, involves making sure airplanes filled with people don't crash. While he's fun loving in his off hours, he's not often the kind of person to play fast and loose with safety.

Naked in the Driveway

Most of the time.

One absolutely gorgeous day, we were all enjoying a great time at the beach, splashing in the water and lounging in the sun with our kids. It was our yearly trip to Australia when our two younger boys get to spend Christmas with my husband's two older boys. When the big boys dug a sizeable hole in the sand, my husband thought it would be a great idea to bury the children.

Being boys, all the kids heartily agreed.

It looked like something out of a grisly execution scene. Crouched on their knees, the kids each held still in their respective holes while we 'responsible' adults buried them up to their necks. When we were done, nothing was left but four blonde heads resting their chins on the beach. Had the boys not been laughing, any innocent passerby might have suspected we'd decapitated them.

It wasn't the first time my husband has had a different idea of what's a good way to play in the water with the kids. I once caught him holding the kids upside down and dunking them in the pool.

They were laughing but I got him to stop when I pointed out that this hilarious pool game was only one small step away from water-boarding, that form of faux drowning made popular in Guantanamo Bay.

This time, though, I was right there with him until we patted down the last handful of sand. Just then, a giant wave rose up and crashed over all the kids' heads.

The next few minutes saw us both frantically unearthing the children, clawing at the loosely packed sand and yanking them to safety before the ocean could finish them. The good news is that the rogue wave was not enough to drown them. And the kids had, after all, begged us to bury them.

The bad news was that we couldn't stop ourselves from laughing and we had to leave the beach shortly after the incident for fear someone might call Child Protective Services and relieve us of the duty for which we were clearly so poorly suited.

And you thought it was just me.

* * *

As much as we love visiting Australia, one of the great things about Abu Dhabi is that it's so kid friendly. Anywhere else in the world, if a child acts naughty or yells in public, strangers have no problem turning up their noses or telling me what a bad mother I am. You can just see them thinking that they would never allow their *own* children to behave like mine.

In Abu Dhabi, however, my kids have to get extraordinarily out of hand before people stop thinking they're cute. I've seen shop clerks and phone company staffers reward the worst sort of behavior with candy and presents.

While I appreciate the generosity, the other day a shop clerk gave each of my two boys a balloon attached to the end of a plastic stick. I would have been less horrified if she'd simply poked their eyes out herself. Instead, the sadist insisted on turning brother against little brother as the balloons were automatically transformed into 'light sabers'.

I had to take the sticks away from the kids before we even left the mall. My youngest cried the tears of true betrayal when the wind blew his balloon away, and my eldest howled with fervor when his popped – we narrowly escaped holding a wake for the floppy remains.

I appreciate the kindness of the clerk, though. I'm sure she assumed that since I was buying them Krispy Kreme doughnuts, all hope was lost for my children and that a couple of balloons on top of a clearly rotten diet couldn't be all that bad.

* * *

It would be no wonder if a shop clerk gave up all hope for my children with one look. If my pets and plants are anything to go by, things are not looking good for my children.

Our one-eyed cat has grown up hating everyone in the world except for me, and that's just because I feed her – no socialization there. I've also managed to kill an entire school of fish, including one we named Steve McQueen because he survived an escape attempt that ended when he landed in the forest of lint behind the buffet table.

Of my two remaining fish, one has apparently lost her will to live and won't rise off the floor of the tank. She just bobs there gasping for bubbles while the other one looks to be growing either a third eye or a horn out the top of his head.

The plants are even worse. My front porch has been the scene of a foliage massacre. Of the field of flowers I bought and had my husband replant into giant terra cotta pots, not one single solitary petal remains alive.

I can only hope my children are more like the nondescript plant that sits on my desk in my office. When I say 'nondescript', I mean that even the guy in the botanical section of grocery store couldn't come up with a genus or species more precise than 'green plant'.

This poor plant gets no direct sunlight – in fact, the only light it *ever* gets is from the halogen bulbs in the ceiling. It sits in the same tiny plastic pot it was in when I bought it, having never been given a proper terra cotta home. I'll forget to water it for days on end and then rabidly overwater it out of guilt, sometimes with the dregs of my herbal tea.

In short I've done nothing to further the life of this living being.

In spite of it all, however, Green Plant thrives, leafy and hearty. Maybe it's the carbon dioxide breathed on it by me and my colleagues that keeps it alive. Maybe it's the clandestine attention of a night time cleaner. Perhaps it's just a genetically tough species.

Whatever it is, if Green Plant can survive me, perhaps Little Boy and Littler Boy have a fighting chance.

* * *

I wouldn't mind (quite so much) being the most scatterbrained, disheveled mom I know, but it doesn't take long to notice that there's a shocking number of really amazing mothers in Abu Dhabi – intelligent, beautiful, talented women who look none the worse for wear after multiple births.

Take my Dutch friend, whose daughter is in my son's kindergarten class. This woman wore her über-stylish size zero clothes out of the hospital after the birth of her second child. Once a hard-hitting lawyer, she now wears five-inch stilettos on the school run. She has a bilingual child who's already reading at the advanced level in her second language and who will eat anything you put in front of her, including broccoli.

My children are not so compliant. At too young an age, I introduced them to the worldly pleasures of McDonalds and Kinder Surprise eggs. If I only packed their lunchboxes with the sort of food I thought they might actually eat, someone would call the police and accuse me of child abuse.

As it is, I could have fed everyone in North America with the amount of food I've put into their lunchboxes knowing full well I'd end up throwing it away at the end of the day. But I pack the fruit anyway. I mean, I can't have their teachers thinking less of me.

These days, I only pack the fruit and vegetables in my kitchen that I need to throw away. Anything that looks reasonably healthy and isn't growing mold goes into those lunchboxes. That way, my children get to relish the pleasure of refusing their food, the teachers blame my wayward kids, I look like a hero for packing four food groups and I get a nice clean refrigerator all at the same time. Problem solved.

* * *

Of course, the whole lunch box situation is a little embarrassing considering how many of the other kids will happily eat raw fruits and vegetables without a qualm. But for all the times I've been embarrassed at the school or the shops, nothing beats taking them to church for a big fat slice of humble pie.

And while I've lost track of the number of times my children have shamed me while we were in church, my most embarrassing moment wasn't their fault.

Not directly, anyway.

I'd spent one very long, very messy weekend night holding my youngest son while he threw up for hours on end. When the sun came up the following morning, I left him sleeping in the care of my husband and took the oldest to church.

Now, I'm all for consistency, but I would have stayed home that day if I hadn't been scheduled to read one of the scriptures in front of the congregation that morning. Bone tired though I was, I didn't want to let down my fellow parishioners. To stave off the exhaustion, I stopped by Starbucks on the way to church and dived right into a colossal sized cafe latte, pumping myself full of caffeine.

By the time it was my turn to read, I was not only dog tired but the coffee had given me a case of the twitches so bad my hands were shaking. Still, I was determined to soldier on.

Despite previous acts of riotous behavior, this morning my darling firstborn silently held my hand, walked to the front of the church and stood motionless beside me behind the podium as I started to read a passage from the Old Testament.

Practically no one else saw another very small boy come toddling down the side aisle, a boy younger than both of mine. As I read, I watched the toddler waddle all the way up to the front of the church. He was reaching for the decorative ministerial stole the preacher was wearing before someone got his attention and lured the child back to his seat.

Standing in front of the entire congregation, I was reminded of a morning a few months before when my own two kids had made a break for the front of the church.

One minute they were only a step away, but the next they were running for the minister – who was in the middle of giving his sermon. My youngest was just reaching to pull the table cloth out from under the communion host and wine when I caught him.

Remembering that morning – when the minister tried to assure me that I was doing well in spite of the obvious evidence to the contrary – the damage was done. Two lines into my Old Testament reading, I was reminded of all the times that it had been *my* kid wandering off, and I got a case of the giggles. The caffeine and sleep deprivation took that giggle and ran with it.

What started as a teeter snowballed into runaway guffaws that eventually affected the entire congregation, everyone giggling along – either amused or horrified or both. When the minister finally asked if I would be able to continue, my own son looked up at me, clearly puzzled and more than a little disappointed.

Somehow I was able to hold my breath and finish, but to this day, it's yet to be seen if our souls will be saved.

* * *

If you think I'm no good at managing my kids in church, I'd also like to publicly admit before God and man that I am a terrible cook. I would like to think I make-up for it in other ways, but other than a few standards, most of what I cook is ordinary at best.

I feel especially bad for my poor husband. I dearly love him – I still have a crush on him and giggle when he calls for no reason – but I completely understand when he describes my food as flavorless and boring. I don't even mind when he douses his entire plate in ketchup or throws on a handful of basil.

For all of his complaining, he's hardly wasting away. He often finishes everything I serve him and sneaks back later for midnight snacks. Still, I feel bad that just about every meal I prepare for him turns out to be a culinary disappointment.

Naked in the Driveway

At least part of my problem is my lack of attention to detail. I once bought an expensive casserole kit and managed to ruin the entire affair by adding a tablespoon of water instead of milk. I've discovered the hard way that, no matter how much ginger paste you add to a curry, it will never taste like garlic and that no matter how long you leave a pot on the stovetop, it will never come to a boil until sometime *after* you've switched the power on.

I keep thinking modern science will eventually bring something to the table to help me but I can't figure out what to do with the three different flavors of Bisto sauce mix in my cupboard. Does it go on before, during or after? And what exactly is it supposed to do anyway?

I guess, though, if I'm going to earn a full-time wage, manage grocery shopping and bill paying, take the kids to football practice and attend parent/teacher conferences all the while saving back just enough energy to have creative, energetic sex with my husband, I can leave gourmet cookery off the list.

* * *

After five years of raising children, you'd think I would have lost my ability to be surprised. I've seen my children tightrope walk the wall that runs along the third floor of our house, hide out from me in the toy section of the biggest shop in town, even sneeze in my face.

But nothing could have prepared me for what my youngest son did this past weekend.

We were at the beach, and my friend and I thought we should get her son to have lunch with my two boys. We were hoping that peer pressure and the spirit of competition would inspire them all to eat and, miraculously, it worked. My two children devoured everything I put in front of them – grilled chicken, brown rice, fruit salad, everything.

It was an amazing sight considering how hard I've had to work on so many occasions to get them to eat anything at all or, more accurately, anything that hasn't been deep fried, air popped or dipped in chocolate.

I would have been happy enough if my kids had merely eaten their own food, but then it happened. My littlest boy – the one with the hardest head, the one most likely to starve himself than eat something he doesn't want – reached for a stalk of broccoli left over on his friend's plate.

And ate the whole thing.

It was more Vitamin C than his little body has absorbed since I finally quit breastfeeding him. I couldn't have been more astounded if he'd started conjugating Latin verbs. A hit of green vegetable like that should have had the same effect on his bloodstream as an adrenaline shot straight to his aorta. I'm amazed he didn't drop dead on the spot.

Which just goes to show that if you play your cards right, you can get childhood rebellion to work for you.

* * *

I'm overjoyed my son has decided broccoli is palatable because it seems I've fed my kids chicken nuggets so often that they're actually sick of them.

For some reason I don't fully understand, the concept of the drive-through window has gone largely overlooked in Abu Dhabi. Between the oppressive heat and masses of children, there *has* to be a market.

I know that, after a day of shopping and running errands, I can always appease (or is that bribe?) my good little children with a couple of Happy Meals, and I'll drive miles out of my way to go to the only McDonalds in town with a drive-through rather than having to take the kids out of their car seats. Again.

Before you write me to complain (and you can! Visit www.laurafulton.org to find out how!) let me clarify that yes, I know McDonalds is bad for them. Yes, I know there are parents who have never allowed the taste of pre-formed chicken nuggets to sully their children's lips.

Before I had kids, I swore that when I did, they were *never* going to eat McDonalds. They were also never going to play video games, have white bread or go to bed without a bath. I was such a good mother before I had kids.

It's not like they eat nothing but junk food. They like strawberries and mango. They like rice. My youngest has finally started to eat those little green trees he calls 'broppoli'. It's just that some days, I absolutely can't face the thought of making one more stop or leaving my kids hungry for the 45 minutes it's going to take for us to get home.

Even better, though my good friend and brilliant educator Jason once described a McDonald's Happy Meal as 'a plate full of scurvy', it turns out there's enough nutrients in a small serving of McDonald's French fries to stave off scurvy.

Of course, how would I know? I mean, aren't their teeth *supposed* to fall out?

Since I've learned to embrace the badness of my mothering, we've worked out a pretty good Happy Meal system for when we're in the car. The apple juices go into the cup holders first so the boys can quench their parched throats while I dump the nuggets and chips directly into the open boxes for easy access.

And if the chicken is too hot, I've discovered they wedge perfectly into the air conditioning vents in my car – I can cool down all eight nuggets at once.

Efficient, yes, but you probably want to test out the size of your vents before you try it. My younger sister learned the hard way when, on my advice, she hurriedly shoved a nugget into the A/C vent of her Jeep Wrangler only to watch, with mouth agape, as it slipped right through and disappear into the bowels of the car.

Apparently, *that* smell is a hard one to explain to the other half. Consider yourself warned.

* * *

Naked in the Driveway

For every moment of their lives I've tried to get my kids to eat, I've spent a parallel moment trying to keep myself from eating. For years, I've tried and failed to cultivate the sort of eating disorder that would leave me waif thin. It turns out, unfortunately, that I have too strong a survival instinct to deprive myself of food for longer than a few hours at a time.

I've recently discovered, however, that I've developed a different kind of disorder – the irrational fear that my sons will reject so much food that they'll starve themselves to death.

I call it 'boyarexia'.

In days of yore, there was no such thing as active, healthy children refusing food. They would be so hungry from deprivation and hard labor that they would happily eat whatever was placed before them. Logic dictates that I should just wait my children out. Sooner or later, they're sure to be so hungry they'll eat their vegetables out of pure starvation.

It worked for my own mother, but only when I was a child. I was forced to eat lots of foods I didn't like, but the moment I left home and was in complete control of my own diet, I spurned vegetables for years, which worked exactly opposite to the theme of healthy eating my mom was trying to instill.

What I need to remember is that my kids' refusal to eat is my own disorder. I don't have to force them to eat something they don't want, but I really must refrain from giving them anything else. I don't have to make it a confrontation, but I must remember that they really will eat when they're hungry.

My mind knows that, but at the ages of three and five, my babies have turned to psychological warfare. They'll refuse their dinner but turn to me with imploring eyes an hour later and say, 'But Mommy, I'm so *hungry!*' and all my soft heart can see is the grubby face of Oliver Twist holding up his empty bowl begging, 'Please, sir, I want some more'.

Tell me that's not a disorder.

* * *

Last week, I had one of those moments every mother dreads. We were watching one of the boys' favorite movies, *Transformers*. Now, I'm hesitant to let the kids watch this fast-paced action movie, mainly because every time we do, I find my two little heroes locked in hand-to-hand combat, re-enacting the most brutal scenes long before the end.

But this day, my oldest son gave me another reason to ban *Transformers* – almost.

Towards the beginning of the film, the slightly geeky protagonist Sam Witwicky (played by Shia LeBeouf) offers a ride to the incredibly gorgeous Mikaela (played by the stunning Megan Fox).

Unbeknownst to Sam, his newly purchased vintage Camaro is actually an alien robot in disguise. When the car pretends to break down, Sam is both baffled and horrified until the sultry Mikaela pulls back her hair and instructs Sam to pop the hood.

In a scene that's sure to go down in the Greatest Car Moments in Movies Hall of Fame, Ms Fox raises the hood of the car and stands peering in, bending just enough to accentuate her backside with her arms stretched up over her head.

The camera angles so that all we see is this stunning sample of the female physique wearing a form-fitting skirt so short it could double as a belt and a scrap of a skintight tank top that perfectly captures the image of her flat, tanned stomach backlit by the setting sun.

Just as I was beginning to wonder how it could be biologically possible for one woman to be that outrageously beautiful, I happened to notice my oldest son. He'd been playing on his own, not really paying attention to the movie, but the minute the hood of the car went up, he stopped.

There stood my five year old, stock still, mouth agape, staring with naked lust at the TV screen. He didn't move until the girl slammed down the hood and got back into the car, and the camera angled to an interior shot. Then, as though he was shell shocked, he spoke.

'Mommy,' he breathed with heartfelt longing. 'I love that car.'

Between a sex kitten and a 1977 Camaro, my son chose the Chevy. If that's not enough to make a mother's heart sing, I don't know what is.

APPENDIX G: STUFF YOU REALLY NEED IN YOUR CARRY-ON WHEN YOU'RE TRAVELLING A LONG WAY WITH KIDS

For you

- Lip balm
- Eye drops
- Panadol
- Spare clothes (or at least spare top in the event you can't find air sick bags and someone spews all over you – not an aroma you want to wear for the remainder of your journey)

For the kids

- Movies and/or handheld video games (unless you're *100 percent* sure the plane will have them, in which case the less heavy stuff you have to carry, the better)

- Coloring books and crayons (*not* markers because they can get everywhere in a hurry and *not* pencils because they don't color very well and the kids will just whine and ask you to find something else for them to do)
- Spare clothes, especially underpants if they're anything less than *100 percent* potty trained (Note: My otherwise steady-handed children are famous for spilling stuff all over themselves within the first five minutes of a flight, so an extra outfit is a *must*)
- Snacks you're *sure* they'll eat (but not too many because – depending on where you are and where you're going – airport security sometimes makes you throw them away)
- A few small toys you wouldn't mind never seeing again, in case they get lost
- Wet wipes and at least one empty plastic bag
- Any medicines you might need in flight

Appendix H: Stuff You Really *Don't* Need in Your Carry-On When You're Travelling a Long Way with Kids

For you

- Any form of entertainment that requires more than 15 percent of your attention at a time
- Make-up (by the time you get to your final destination, you're going to look like you've been dragged through the bushes backwards – if your family and friends don't love you enough to see you without make-up, reconsider

spending your money on a spa retreat instead of an airline ticket)
- Clothes you don't want to see defiled with vomit, snot, food or other human fluids

For the kids

- Toys with small parts or pieces that can get lost
- Toys your kids absolutely can't live without (unless you're willing to look after those toys with as much diligence as you look after your kids – which may or may not be that much)
- Clothes you couldn't throw away in an airplane bathroom in the event of a bowel, stomach or other digestive catastrophe
- Really heavy stuff or messy stuff

Note: If it's within your means and your kids are old enough, I highly recommend getting an iPad (or two or three) loaded up with movies, music, books, games and other stuff to keep yourself and the kids entertained – perfect for the airplane or for long layovers in boring airports. Just don't forget the charger and a power adapter if you're travelling internationally.

A WHOLE PACK OF HASSLE

If I haven't made it abundantly clear so far, let me just say once again that travelling with kids can be a bit of a trick, especially when I'm on my own. In fact, the only thing worse than travelling with two small kids by myself is doing it in the United States.

After so many years living in the UAE, I've come to accept that when it comes to air travel, I've been completely spoiled. The most cost effective airlines in this part of the world – heavy hitters like Singapore Airlines, Emirates Airlines and Qatar Airways – employ flight attendants who are genuinely friendly and dote on my children.

It's not just the air hostesses, though. The entire airline industry in this part of the world makes an effort to accommodate children and families. Most flights are on planes that provide televisions for every individual seat (even in economy) and a selection of movies and TV programs geared towards a variety of ages and interests. As soon as the kids are seated, they get special toys and gifts to entertain them.

The airlines also make sure to seat people with kids in such a way that they minimize the inconvenience for both parents and non-parents. There are ways of grouping passengers that keep the kids together and the rest of the world out of their way.

Flying in the continental United States, however, is an entirely different kettle of bottom feeders.

Often, during Abu Dhabi's sweltering summer, I take my boys to visit my family in Arkansas while my husband stays behind to work. Trying to save money last year, we signed on for one of the first flights of an American airline (*not* American Airlines) that had started to fly directly into the UAE. In their effort to drum up business for the route, they'd priced the flight attractively low, so we decided to go for it.

'How bad could it be?' we foolishly thought. I must remember to strike those words in that particular order from my vocabulary.

Instead of having enough televisions for everybody to have their own, this plane was equipped with exactly six screens that were meant to entertain the entire economy class for the duration of the first eight-hour leg of our journey. The programs they *did* screen were only of marginal interest to the adults on the flight and of no interest at all to the kids.

Now, I'd come prepared with a portable DVD player but discovered almost immediately that all the time I'd had it plugged in before we left, the device had not, in fact, been collecting a charge. Either through a poor connection or some error on my part, it hadn't charged at all so it was completely useless for anything other than toning my upper back muscles as one more thing to carry in my backpack.

For awhile, it didn't matter. Though they were only two and four years old at the time, the boys hung in there marvelously for most of our hours in the air. They played with their toys and looked at books, slept a little and had their snacks. After an eight-hour flight followed by a four-hour layover in Germany, however, all the fun of air travel was gone for them.

Boarding in Frankfurt for the second leg of our journey, the lesson in humiliation began.

Now, newborn infants are pretty easy to travel with. They can't wander off, they're not able to roll out of the wall-mounted bassinet and provided you give them something to suck on, my boys at least were pretty quiet when they were tiny.

The toddler years were harder. Between the ages of one and three, my boys weren't able to sit still for very long and would spend entire flights running the aisles of whatever aircraft would have us. I spent many long hours walking laps around planes, hoping to wear out my children.

But by this journey, they were old enough to travel reasonably well again. There was no mindless screaming or running and I thought they were going to make it – until, that is, the seatbelt sign came on long before it was time for us to land.

Through no choice of our own, we'd been given the row of seats at the very back of the plane next to the toilets, the crappy ones that don't recline. What small amount of space we had allotted to us was decreased that bit further when the people in the seats in front of us insisted on cranking back their seats as far as they would go for the entire flight.

Now, as a mother, I know exactly how annoying it is when a kid keeps kicking the back of your seat (it happens often in the car), and I can only imagine how much more annoying it would be if the child in question wasn't the actual fruit of your own personal loins.

I contend, though, that if you're going to cut into the meager few inches I have between me and your seat when you're *not even sleeping*, I will encourage my children to kick you all they want.

In all honesty, I tried to make my youngest stop. I knew the woman sitting directly in front of my two year old hated all of us bitterly but the surly flight attendants had told me in no uncertain terms that I had to keep my son in his seatbelt.

I could punish him, but I knew that anything I did to dissuade the kicking would make him scream which would invariably annoy everyone within earshot of us rather than just that one woman.

My logic was this – I couldn't smack my son for fear the air marshals would arrest me on the spot, so surely our fellow traveler couldn't kill us for the same reason.

Obviously if I was a better parent, my kids would simply do as I said, regardless of their ages or the circumstances, but what could I do? *Not* take them to see my parents just once a year? It's not the kids' fault that they were born in the UAE and that all of their relatives live 16 hours away in opposite directions.

All things considered, I thought they'd done as well as they could. No one threw up, no one had a nose bleed and no one had diarrhea. A little seat-kicking and uninhibited laughing were small crimes indeed compared to the havoc they could have wrecked.

The flight crew, however, disagreed and told me so.

Apparently, the sadistic ground crew who chose our seats weren't trying to punish *me* by sticking us in the worst seats on the entire plane. Clearly those evil ladies had it in for their colleagues in the sky.

'This is our *only sleeping area*,' growled the angriest air hostess I've ever encountered, pointing to a grey plastic sheet curtaining off the last two rows of seats opposite the aisle from us. 'I only get a few hours to sleep, and I wasn't able to sleep the *entire way* because your children have been making so much noise.'

There were so many things I could have said to her in response that I didn't, including:

- 'Wow, this airline doesn't provide very good accommodation for you guys, does it?'

- 'I feel your pain – I haven't slept in over 24 hours'

- 'If sleeping is that important to you, you should tell the ground staff to seat children further away from your *only sleeping area*'

- 'We're doing the best we can – did you notice they're laughing, not screaming?'

- 'Your life sucks, sister. Have you considered another line of work?'

Instead, I took a deep breath, smiled and apologized. When I told her that my children were in their 18th hour of this journey and that we were barely half way, however, she straightened right up. Confronted with a pair of preschoolers who were better travelers than she was, despite her profession, she offered us a DVD player from business class (which also hadn't been charged properly) and brought the kids ice cream.

I haven't forgiven her yet, but I'm working on it.

* * *

Appendix I: Other Things I've Wanted to Say to Flight Attendants at One Time or Another but Didn't

- If you're going to rub your boobs against my husband's arm like that, I really must insist you move us all to business class

- Just because I'm enormously pregnant doesn't mean I can't see you flirting with the father of my children – I'm actually still standing *right here*

- *Of course* I'm not bitter that you're taller, younger and prettier than I am and that you actually *are* in my husband's league

- Can you please ask the asshole in front of me to put up his damn seat back so that I can put down my tray table and have a meal? He's been awake for hours farting and there's no one sitting in front of him and even though I've had a loud conversation with my husband about what a dickhead he is, he's just not responding

- Did you just kick my toddler in the face? I know he's crawling around on the filthy floor of this airplane, but what would you prefer I do? Hold him for 12 hours and make everyone in the surrounding 50 rows listen to him scream? Or let him crawl in silence? Let's take a poll of all the people sitting in the surrounding 50 rows. Oh, better not – they're sleeping

- You're doing an amazing job. I'm sorry that your position as 'person in charge of seeing us to safety in the event of an accident' has been relegated to 'waitress who doesn't get tips'. I really truly couldn't do your job

- As a matter of fact, I'd love more wine (OK, I *have* said this one)

* * *

When it came time for us to make our Christmas trip to Australia a few months later, I had the advantage of travelling with my husband and with an airline that has a clearer understanding of the concept of customer service.

Despite the team effort between my husband and I, it ended up being one of the worst travel disasters of either of our lives. There are several factors we could blame for what went wrong but I suspect it's all down to one.

It might have been a giant karmic smack down. We had won an Audi TT almost exactly a year before after buying only two raffle tickets, and that sort of good luck can't be left lying around without something to balance it out.

It might also have been our general lack of concern for the entire trip. Having made the same trek so many times before, an international journey with two kids doesn't seem like a big deal anymore. This time, I would at least have my husband travelling with me in confirmed seats the entire way. We both thought to ourselves, 'What could possibly go wrong?' with a careless 'Pshaw!'.

It's even very likely that, after the debacle of the standby trip to Cudgee the year before, I actually said the words out loud: 'Well, it couldn't be worse than last year.' Of course, *those* words would come back to haunt me.

Personally, though, I blame the comfort pack.

The name makes me think a comfort pack should contain a fifth of whisky, a bottle of hand lotion and a paper towel.

In fact, a comfort pack is one of many items available for purchase on Air Asia, the newest low-cost airline to grace the skies of this half of the world. In exchange for staying at least 12 hours in Malaysia, travelers can buy reasonably priced tickets that will take them from Abu Dhabi as far as London to the west and all the way to Melbourne to the east.

Ever the travel genius, my husband thought we would all enjoy a night in Malaysia to break up the long flight to Melbourne. That we got our tickets for a great price was practically a bonus, he had argued. Ever faithful, I agreed.

We made the flight from Abu Dhabi to Kuala Lumpur without incident. Sure there were none of the usual bells and whistles that accompany most international flights but we were prepared. We had our own portable DVD player (properly charged this time), plenty of movies and snacks and the smug attitude of people who have saved a lot of money.

In an effort to keep costs down, Air Asia doesn't provide pillows and blankets, but for the bargain price of 25 ringgits (a little less than $8), passengers can purchase a comfort pack which contains not the ingredients for pleasuring one's self but instead a micro-fiber blanket, an inflatable neck pillow and a kidney-shaped eye mask.

Now, my husband and I have first-hand experience being middle class. We both grew up wearing hand-me-down clothes and calling annual visits to relatives 'holidays', so when we formed the Fulton Family Frugal Duo, we figured we were unstoppable. No throwing away the equivalent of $7.50 on a neck pillow for us.

The woman sitting in front of us, however, had no such qualms. She, in fact, was apparently so flush with cash that she not only purchased the comfort pack, but actually left it behind on the plane. It seemed almost sinfully wasteful to my husband and me. We're the sort of people who always take the free shampoo and lotion from hotel room bathrooms since they are, after all, rightfully ours.

Walking down the aisle on our way to disembark, we picked up the discarded comfort pack, reassembled it in the little bag in which it came and stuffed it into my husband's backpack.

For a moment, we thought we should probably chase down the woman and clarify whether or not she actually *meant* to leave her comfort pack behind, but while we hesitated, we lost her in the crowd and we carefully managed not to see her again at baggage claim.

Later, we would be sorry.

* * *

We opted to spend our twelve hours in Malaysia on the way to Australia instead of on the way home, and in general, I recommend breaking up a long trip with a bit of down time. We spent a lovely late afternoon swimming in the pool, and after ordering room service, we all enjoyed a reasonably good night's sleep.

After breakfast the next morning, we loaded up two suitcases, two backpacks, two kids and one stroller onto the bus that would take us to the airport. What happened next is the sort of mistake only a seasoned, jaded traveler would make.

'You just look after the kids,' my husband barked, snatching a suitcase out of my hand as we arrived at the international airport. 'I'll look after the luggage.'

Instead of pulling up directly alongside the curb, the bus driver had stopped a fair distance from the sidewalk so that we had to walk through a small parking lot to get out of the road.

If I had been first off the bus, I could have commandeered both children myself, so the whole thing is partly my fault. As it was, my husband stood blocking the aisle and our youngest hopped off the bus leaving my husband to hoist the luggage out of the way before he could chase after our son.

Now, the kind, elderly woman who took our little son by the hand and started walking away with him was almost certainly trying to be helpful. She almost certainly saw that we had our hands full and only wanted to see our sweet, innocent child safely out of the road.

But in that moment of unloading and preparing to fly and people scurrying everywhere, my husband saw the back of his youngest son walking away in the hand of a stranger and panicked.

As nicely as possible, he ran ahead and snatched back our son, then returned to the luggage.

It was only a split second mistake. My husband took the suitcases off the bus, threw them onto a luggage trolley, grabbed back the wayward child, plopped him into the stroller and away we went. It took my husband about a dozen steps to realize that, while we had two suitcases, two children and one stroller, we only had one backpack - the one I had not taken off my person since putting it on that morning.

'Laura!' he asked in abject despair. 'Where's my backpack?'

'On your back, I would assume,' I retorted. I might have been more sympathetic if he hadn't been so snarky with me as we were getting off the bus.

Now, it's important to remember that when I met my husband one of the first things he said to me was that he was an air traffic *controller*, so I should know what to expect. Back in Abu Dhabi the day before, when I suggested that I carry my own passport and the pair of passports for one of our dual-nationality children in my backpack, he disagreed.

'All of those documents are very important and if you carry them, you might lose them,' he'd condescended. You would think he would know better by now, but when I pressed the issue, he uttered the Mantra of Doom.

'For God's sake, Laura, it's just passports. You act like it's such a big deal.'

And so we packed *all* the passports into his backpack – the one still sitting in the public bus we stood watching as it drove away from the Kuala Lumpur International Airport.

Almost everything important we had between the two of us was lost, including my new jacket, our portable DVD player, our much-loved copy of the Mike Meyers movie *The Cat in the Hat* and the $1000 in Australian cash that we'd had exchanged for the trip.

The worst of all, we lost all six of our passports, the passports bearing the residence visas that allow us to live and work in the UAE.

There was no time for judgment or blame. After a two-hour chase, my husband caught up with the bus. In light of our indiscretion with the comfort pack, neither of us was surprised to find the backpack had been stolen.

There was nothing we could do, so we changed our flights and set out to navigate the bureaucratic wilderness that would get us out of Malaysia, into Australia and back to Abu Dhabi again.

Our first order of business was to prioritize. Since three of the four of us had Australian passports and we were destined for Australia, we made the Australian embassy our first stop only to discover they are only open from 9.00am to 11.00am each day, about the same hours as the American embassy. It was time to give up for the night, so we headed into town.

* * *

Having made such a generous contribution to the Malaysian economy in the form of my husband's lucrative backpack, we really *had* to save some money. We found a cheap hotel in a bustling part of town, but it was so sketchy we were afraid to put the kids into what had to be the filthiest bathtub in Asia.

After a quick wander in the neighborhood near our hotel, we gave in and had comfort food at the nearby Outback Steakhouse, where a gallon of beer between my husband and me rekindled our spirits.

By the time we got back to the hotel, we were in a pretty good mood, so when we opened the door of our grotty hotel room, we were stunned to see that our luggage had been inexplicably moved across the room.

'Wait,' I said, taking a closer look. 'Those aren't our bags.'

'This isn't our room at all,' my husband observed.

Small wonder our 'key' had worked. It was nothing more than a flat piece of metal that worked about like a credit card can be used to pop a lock. It was funny but more than a little disturbing.

With plans to stay for only one night, we were sort of sad to miss out on what looked to be a very funky part of Kuala Lumpur. Unable to resist a glimpse at the nightlife, my husband went for a quick wander down our street while I stayed with the kids who were both asleep in bed.

When he told me about it later, we couldn't decide which was best. There were fish spas where you could submerge your feet in a giant tank and have tiny fish nibble all the dead skin off of your feet, a cafe named Porkalicious and plenty of ladies standing outside the 'massage parlors' who flirted shamelessly with my husband as he walked by.

'Sir want massage? Very happy ending,' they called to him. 'I give you discount, you so handsome.'

When he was finally ready for bed, it took a team effort to outsmart our decrepit, sloping mattress. Thankfully, we had just enough pillows to keep our heads higher than our feet and we slept the night only a little worried another hotel guest might come into our room by mistake.

The next day, the kids and I started at the US embassy while my husband went back to the Australian embassy. After a quick wait during which the security guards yelled at the kids, I was able to see the US citizen services representatives. One glance at their monitors confirmed that we were who we said we were, and our agent treated us with kindness and sympathy, which was nice.

The four of us regrouped at the nearby twin Petronas Towers shopping mall to get some lunch and the passport-sized photos we would need to get emergency passports from both embassies. After a quick bite, we took an hour to see Santa. We'd planned to visit The Big Man once we'd gotten to Australia but with the way things were going, we couldn't guarantee we'd get the chance before Christmas morning.

Having lived their whole lives in Abu Dhabi, our kids had never seen a truly authentic Santa. The surly version of Mr. Claus serving his sentence at Petronas Towers, though clearly of Asian descent, was the first fat Kris Kringle our kids had ever seen. After holding our spot at the front of the line with much elbowing and ill will towards a whole herd of children set on seeing Santa before us, we finally got our photo op.

While our Santa may have been the portly fellow of legend, he had exactly zero people skills. Instead of asking the kids what they wanted for Christmas, he just sat staring blankly straight ahead, ringing the hell out of a massive bell without so much as a sliver of a smile on his rotund, bearded face.

Having been coached previously, my oldest son took it upon himself to volunteer what both he and his brother wanted for Christmas, but if Santa heard him at all over the ringing of the concussive bell, he gave no indication.

* * *

Upstairs we rushed to get our photos taken, and I was presented with what might be the worst picture that has ever been taken of me.

There was simply nothing that could be done with my hair. My preholiday cut could only be described as a mullet, a cross between something Barbara Brady would wear and an explosion of the atomic bomb. It had been a good idea on the surface but the final result was ultimately wrong on every level. The only thing for it was a ponytail, one that had fallen into disarray in the subtropical humidity.

Horrible photos in hand, we returned to the US embassy with just enough time to get our temporary passports.

As we waited, the children developed a dangerous fascination with the standing fan that struggled to keep the pressing heat at bay. With exactly no time to rush either child to the emergency room for finger reconstruction surgery, I instituted a new Fulton family rule: what gets chopped off in Malaysia stays in Malaysia.

With all we'd been through so far, I was fully prepared to go home with stumpy children.

The people at the Australian embassy were inordinately helpful, giving us all kinds of useful tips and information. Soon all four of us were ready to continue on. Though we were set to get into Australia and back into Abu Dhabi (we thought), the agents at the Australian embassy let us know that we wouldn't be allowed to leave Malaysia without proper documentation.

The temporary visas that had allowed us to enter the country were tucked safely inside our passports – all of which were gone.

Visits to two embassies turned out to be nothing compared to the nightmare of the Malaysian immigration department an hour outside of town. It took us three hours of waiting while every one of 15 different officials took their turn stamping, signing, stapling and stacking a number of documents in a language we couldn't understand.

As the sun began to set, we finally headed back to town with emergency passports and four massive packets of papers that would allow us to leave the country.

* * *

With one last night in town, we decided to see a bit of the city. Just down the street from our crappy hotel, we tried our first meal of Malaysian food. We figured it probably wasn't the best time to find out whether or not our youngest was allergic to shellfish but we rolled the dice anyway with no ill effect.

Even better, my husband commandeered the children while I went to the fish spa. If laughter is the best medicine, you've got to give this bizarre treatment a try. The theory is that the fish will eat away any dead skin leaving the living skin unharmed, but the nibbling of the fishy mouths was so tickly I laughed out loud the entire thirty minutes I sat with my feet in the water.

We arrived at the airport the next day completely rested but ready to get on with it. It wasn't until I went to change my youngest son's diaper that I discovered that all of our wet wipes had also been in the stolen backpack – along with our comfort pack. Thankfully, it didn't become an issue for the remainder of our quiet, daytime flight.

And so it was we were finally destined for Australia. We finally arrived at our holiday house late on Christmas Eve, relieved that we had gotten to see Angry Santa after all.

* * *

The Curse of the Comfort Pack made its final assault when we arrived back in Abu Dhabi. Like everything else that had been in the backpack, our UAE residence visas were gone. Now, both the US and Australian embassies in Malaysia had been able to identify us with just a few clicks of the keyboard so we assumed the same would be true when we returned home.

We knew the immigration officials in Abu Dhabi could see our photos. Their system, like most others in the world, includes face recognition software, so they knew we were who we said we were. Even though we had emergency passports from two different embassies and a Malaysian police report to prove we'd been robbed, they refused us entry, cancelling our visas.

After nine years of working and residency, we could only come in on tourist visas and start the entire process over again from the beginning as though we'd never set foot in the UAE before.

In the end, our purloined comfort pack turned out to be a discomfort pack.

Guess we had *that* coming.

THE BACK SIDE OF FOUR

It's June 3 and this morning my refrigerator is full to overflowing with leftovers from my youngest son's fourth birthday yesterday.

Shockingly, I managed to pull together two pretty good parties yesterday. This year, all the other moms in my youngest son's class have put on parties at the school rather than inviting everyone to an off-site location, which I think is pretty civilized.

Not so for my older son. He turned five last September, and the parents of his classmates have thrown some massive events this year. The last party we went to was at a popular play centre in one of the shopping malls, complete with an hour on the massive climbing frames followed by games, music, dancing, food and cake in the party room.

Between the throbbing rap music and flashing disco ball, the last hour of the party started to look like a basement rave. It's enough to make all the parents contemplate suicide but the kids loved it. My son even won a prize for dancing.

By the end, I was pretty sure the cute 20 year old girls hosting the party on behalf of the play centre were going to start handing out Ecstasy. Any minute, I was sure poles were going to drop from the ceiling and they would strip out of their skinny jeans to give us a real show.

If I can just clarify, the birthday boy was turning five.

So I've been pretty pleased with the reasonable parents of my younger son's friends until two weeks ago when he came home from school with the party bag he got from his friend's in-class party.

Some overly enthusiastic mom – probably jacked up on green tea and post-yoga endorphins – had gone and *made costumes by hand* for all the kids in the class.

What. An. Asshole.

Striking fear into the hearts of all the other parents and content to make us look like jerks, this mother crafted for my son a shield and a helmet complete (with a sparkly hand-made feather) then modeled a balloon into a sword so that my son could play the part of a knight.

Seriously? How much time can one woman have on her hands?

The joke, in the end, though, was on her. Sure she made a pretty authentic costume but by decorating the shield with a giant red cross and the helmet with a gold one, my son wasn't just a knight but a Crusader, which I thought was a little inappropriate considering we're living in a country in which the majority of our fellow residents are Muslim.

That ought to teach her.

* * *

In light of the costume party, I was pretty pleased with the Africa party I whipped up in honor of my younger son turning four. I made cupcakes topped with jungle animal sugar decorations, bought zebra masks for all the kids to wear, packed little plastic jungle animals in their party bags and invited them all to dance a few vigorous rounds to Shakira's 'Waka Waka'.

OK, so, I made the cupcakes from a mix that came out of a box, topped them with frosting that came out of a can and decorated them with sugar animals I only found at the grocery store by accident. Finding the zebra masks was nothing more than a stroke of luck, the jungle animals were only about 25 cents apiece and the Shakira CD was already in my car.

Some people might call that 'lazy' but I like to say 'efficient'.

Instead, I put in the real time preparing more food than any one party of people could possibly consume for the home celebration for friends and family. While my husband manned the barbeque grill, I put out chips, dips, a fruit platter, spring rolls and vegetables for the sake of the superior parents in attendance whose children actually like vegetables.

Of course, I forgot to buy tomatoes, lettuce or onions for the burgers and we forgot to serve the potato salad, bean medley and baked potatoes we'd prepared, but all in all, the party went down like gangbusters.

This morning sees my boys gleefully cruising the driveway on their new shiny red bicycles. A better mother would probably make the older boy wait till his birthday in three months from now before giving him his bike, but they've never had new bikes before and I just couldn't stand the thought.

Watching the boys play, I'm reminded of a woman I met just a few weeks ago. When I told her the name of the magazine I write for, she asked if I was 'that grumpy mom who writes that stupid column'.

If you've gotten the impression that I'm a negative person or down on my kids, I'd like to take this opportunity to clarify. See, when I was pregnant with my first son and delirious with joy, time and again I encountered a certain subsection of angry older mothers I liked to call the Just You Waiters.

'Just you wait,' they would warn me with a knowing cackle. 'Just you wait until you're so tired you can't think straight, when you've got Caesarean scars and stretch marks, when you're worn down with worry and your house is a mess. You won't be so overjoyed then.'

There's no denying that they were right. My stomach survived two pregnancies more or less intact, but it's true that I spent a lot of months so tired I thought I would never feel rested again. I have aged more in the last six years than I would have if I'd never had kids. I have scribbles on my walls and gray hairs and I often feel unsure of myself.

And then this morning, I woke up to find my little one curled up in bed behind me, his arm around my waist, and my big one curled up under my chin, his hand resting on my cheek.

It was a tiny little throw away moment, over in five minutes, one I won't remember in a week, a month, ten years from now. But it was enough to remind me of all the years I spent before they came into my life, all the nights I spent lying in bed alone, crying myself to sleep, certain I would never find this much love all in one spot, all for me.

Yeah, being a mom is hard work but just so you know, I wouldn't have missed it for the world.

* * *

In fact, now that the boys are growing up, I'm starting to feel the first tugs of regret for every moment I wished their babyhoods away. Just a few weeks ago, I saw my oldest graduate from kindergarten and the little one from nursery school. They were two days I never want to forget.

Now, my main job at the moment is writing for a magazine, but more than once in the interest of saving time and manpower, I've also served as a photographer.

Unlike drawing up lists and making fun of myself (both of which I do pretty well), photography is not my strong suit. Part of the reason I sometimes don't get the shot I want, though, is down to my peers in the industry.

Unlike the very patient and talented guy who takes most of the pictures for the magazine I write for, the vast majority of the professional photographers in Abu Dhabi are a cutthroat, remorseless bunch ready to shove, elbow and gouge to get the prime spot at a press conference.

However ruthless Abu Dhabi's professional photographers may be, they're a choir of singing angels compared to the group I saw last week. There's no photographer more lethal than a parent trying to get the money shot of their baby graduating from nursery school.

As the first class of wee graduates came filing in wearing mortarboard caps made from construction paper, the foyer of my son's nursery turned into a scene right out of the WWE as moms in Capri pants kicked the pumps right out from under the mothers of their kids' classmates, scrambling to capture the moment.

OK, I'm kidding. I was probably the worst of the lot.

I can't say with any certainty that I actually body checked anyone, but I do know that after pushing past all the other misty-eyed parents, in every shot I took my son is staring into the distance, vacant and slack jawed with his tongue out.

I know I will treasure that day.

My oldest son was even worse. While my youngest stood staring into space for the duration of his graduation ceremony, my oldest took his place on the risers in front of all the other parents with fingers from both hands in his mouth at the same time.

He still made me proud, though, when he went to collect his certificate that documented him as a kindergarten graduate. As each child approached, the teacher asked what they wanted to be when they grew up.

Most of the girls said they wanted to be a teacher and several of the boys said they wanted to be a race car driver. My son was the only one in the class to say he wanted to be a boxer.

Well, why not?

* * *

As my boys grow older, there are certain moments from their childhoods I doubt I'll ever forget.

When they were toddlers, for example, both of my boys went through a phase of stripping off all their clothes pretty much on a whim. It was nothing unusual for me to send them outside to play for the afternoon dressed in t-shirts and shorts only to find them an hour later jumping on the trampoline in full view of the neighbors wearing nothing but a smile, their bits and bobs bouncing in the breeze.

My mother-in-law tells me they're only following in their father's footsteps.

Naked in the Driveway

When he was only three years old, my husband decided to go visit his friends, the people who lived at the nearest farm five kilometers down the road. His mother was even more distracted than I am – in addition to raising five kids all born within a few years of each other, she also pulled her weight running the family dairy farm on the south coast of Australia.

When the neighbor in question called her to ask her if she knew where her only son was, she assumed he was where he always was: 'around here somewhere'.

She was only sort of surprised when she learned that the boy who would grow up to be my husband had ridden his tricycle on his own to the neighbor's house. She was maybe a little more surprised when she heard that he'd made the trip and was now sitting at the table in her neighbor's kitchen drinking chocolate milk – and wearing nothing but a pair of red rubber boots.

It wasn't the first time. My future mother-in-law recalls another day when visitors came to their house and found the boy that would someday become my beloved up a tree in his bare essentials. The visitor kindly pointed out that if she wanted to have someone to carry on the family name, she might want to get him out of the tree.

Talk about a family tradition.

* * *

For some reason I don't fully understand, my boys are fascinated by tiny babies. They're certainly not effeminate, and I can say *that* with conviction (although I would love them just the same if they were). In addition to their loves of all things vehicular, they're also fans of every single super hero there is, including the weird and flimsy ones like the Power Rangers and the redheaded guy with the green ring.

They both love running around getting sweaty, they love digging in the dirt and if a bully has it in mind to pick on either one of them, he's pretty likely to regret that decision post haste. They're more than willing to throw themselves into hand-to-hand combat and neither will hesitate to resort to raw pugilism to settle conflicts between them.

Yeah, we're working on it.

For all the raging testosterone surging through their little bodies, both of my boys think infants are pretty amazing. Recently, we visited my cousin and her newest baby who was born less than two months ago. As I sat on the sofa holding the tiny little girl on my lap, my youngest son came and sat down beside me to investigate.

He'd spent several minutes stroking the baby's head and feet and kissing her when my aunt asked the worst sort of leading question.

'Would you like a new baby at your house?' she asked my youngest son, cutting me a wicked glance.

My son looked at her, looked at me and then looked back at her with knowing, deadpan eyes.

'Even we don't have a dog at our house,' he sighed, with the world-weary knowledge that if his mean, cruel parents won't get him a dog, they're even less likely to produce another baby.

Got *that* right, mister.

* * *

Though they're not likely to get any more siblings, my sons are well on their way to making their own babies.

One day last week, my oldest son complained that he didn't want to go to summer camp. When I asked him why, he sighed, 'Everybody doesn't like me yet.'

It goes without saying, he's sure, that given enough time, everybody will like him – but with the revolving door of kids coming and going throughout the summer, he's had to restructure his clique of homies every week. Apparently the effort of coming up with all the charm and charisma to make everybody like him each week is wearing him out.

I'm glad that he's accustomed to being liked, but sometimes it can be a bit of a pain in the backside. Last year, as we were getting ready to make our annual trip to Australia, he got yet another invitation to a birthday party.

'Crap!' I thought. 'If he were more awkward and less socially capable, we'd save a fortune in presents!'

Although I didn't mind buying the present, I was rather pressed for time. Since it looked as though every kid in the class had been invited to the party, I thought I should clarify my son's relationship with the birthday girl. If they weren't close, maybe we could skip the party.

'Hey, babe, who's Kristy?' I asked him, for once hoping to get a blank stare.

'She's in my class.'

'Are you friends with her? Like, do you play with her a lot?'

'Because Mommy, we're getting married,' he said in that tone of voice that says *der, are you stupid?*

Well, it sounded serious - perhaps they'd undergone some playground betrothal ritual to which I had not been privy? There was nothing for it but to pick out a gift and go along.

At the shop, my son had a very clear understanding of what he thought young Kristy might like. She, it seemed, had been thoughtful enough to provide her young fiancé with several suggestions - which was selfless on her part, I thought, considering how many women expect their partners to intuitively know what they want.

At the party, the kids all played and when I mentioned to Kristy's mother her daughter's impending nuptials, neither my son nor his beloved denied the relationship.

So imagine my surprise when, just a week later, my son came home with devastating news.

'Because Mommy, Kristy is getting married to Benjamin.'

What? Benjamin?!? A child who doesn't know his letters and dropped out of football to take up *karate*? Clearly there's no way Benjamin comes *close* to holding a candle to my superior progeny. And Kristy? What sort of girl not only breaks off an engagement but turns around and saddles up with a lesser boy *only a week later?* What! A! Whore!

Yeah, OK, so, I'll accept that all the parties in question are only five years old.

But still.

* * *

It's no surprise Kristy's moral compass is pointing straight towards hell – I mean look at her role models, all those Disney heroines with dependency issues and the tramps on the radio singing songs about various forms of sluttery.

But don't get me started on Barbie.

The folks who made the *Toy Story* movies would have us believe that Barbie is still the same wholesome girl Mattel brought to us in the 1950s, only more educated and accomplished. I'll admit Barbie has taken up gainful employment in a number of professions in the course of her long life, including Nurse in a Very Short Skirt, Teacher in a Very Short Skirt and Doctor in a Very Short Skirt and Hip-Length Lab Coat.

You'd be inclined to believe she's done well for herself, considering she's living in the dream house and driving a convertible and all, but I'd like to take this opportunity to make a couple of salient observations.

For one, it's obvious from her résumé that she can't hold down a job for longer than a holiday season, and her relationship with Ken is ambiguous at best – I don't recall the two of them ever getting married. So where is her money coming from? I mean, when you were a kid, did you ever play with Mourning-the-Death-of-My-Millionaire-Father-Who-Left-Me-His-Fortune Barbie?

Yeah, neither did I.

And I'll tell you what else. The original Barbie was introduced at a time when short skirts were all the rage and she's never given up her tendency towards showing off her unnaturally long thin legs and fair enough – I'm not bitter. Very much. So I won't give her too hard a time for sticking with her signature look.

But the last time I went Barbie shopping, looking for a gift for my friend's daughter, I was astounded at what I found.

Barbie – that 'clean-living' girl with both a medical degree *and* a teaching certification – was wearing hipster pants cut so low she must have had a Brazilian bikini wax (which is especially dangerous for a plastic doll) and a crop top so tiny it didn't even cover her entire rib cage.

And it wasn't bad enough that she was showing off her midriff for all the world to see. At some stage, probably between quitting her job as a pediatrician and taking up her career as a NASCAR racing driver, she's gone and gotten a tattoo of a butterfly so gigantic that it covers her entire stomach. It's obvious to me that all those 'careers' are just a cover.

Clearly, Barbie is funding her lavish lifestyle by working as a high dollar call girl.

I mean, if you're old enough to wear hipsters with crop tops and get midriff tattoos, you're too old to be playing with Barbie dolls. That blonde-haired, blue-eyed plastic temptress is sitting on store shelves teaching a whole generation of little girls that not only should they be dangerously thin but that they should also dress for the oldest profession in the history of testosterone.

It's no wonder poor Kristy is already such a little gold digger.

* * *

Now *my* mother – talk about setting an example. For all the mistakes I make as a mother, I really have no good excuse because my mom was a legendary parent.

There was no question about whether or not we would eat vegetables – it was a given that they would be served in appropriate portions with every meal. Choosing to leave those vegetables on the plate uneaten was not an option.

This was a woman who didn't just sew our clothes. She outfitted our Barbie dolls with a handmade trousseau of appropriate garments. A lot of moms are great, but mine once knitted a Barbie ball gown. Beat that.

For all the things she was able to do, I might be most impressed with what she wasn't as good at. My grandfather was a cotton farmer, so even though their farm was within earshot of all the kids playing in the local swimming pool, my mom and her brothers and sister spent their summers wearing blisters on their hands with a hoe chopping weeds from between the cotton stalks.

In fact, she didn't learn to swim until I was in high school and she returned to university to finish the degree she'd forgone in favor of raising me and my sisters.

One of her college graduation requirements was to fulfill a course in physical education. Now, this was a woman who had earned full marks in every class she ever took. A lesser woman might have signed up for a course she knew she could master, like badminton or bowling, but my mother enrolled in swimming.

Because she'd never been taught to swim, my mom grew up with a deep fear of the water. Unlike the rest of her university classmates, who were proficient swimmers on the first day of the course, my mom learned each step in the process from her instructor, from blowing bubbles in the water to floating on her back to each proper stroke.

Her final exam was a real test for her in a way that it wasn't for the others. All half her age, the rest of the class finished their required laps in half the time it took my mom. They all loved her, though, and stood on the side of the pool cheering for her as she doggedly paddled her lane.

Her streak of perfect marks ended at the top of the high diving board. Though she was determined to swallow her terror and jump, her instructor saw how much she was struggling and forbade her.

Instead of the A she was used to earning, she ended up with an unremarkable C but for myself, I was more proud of her C in swimming than I was with all of her more easily won As.

That's what a role model should be – not some trollop with a belly tattoo.

* * *

Despite the betrayal of that tramp Kristy, most of the time young love is sweet. Last week, my youngest came home from summer camp wearing a broken SpongeBob SquarePants wristwatch, a token of affection from a girl who had been in his group that day. True love, no doubt.

And while my oldest son came home from kindergarten on the last day of school two months ago with a love letter in his bag from a girl named Mary, I'm pretty sure I've got a few years before he'll be sneaking off to pleasure himself. Or her.

In the car on the way home that day, he was fishing around in his backpack for a toy when he came upon the letter.

'Oh yeah. Here, Mommy – this is for you.'

Now, I know my kids' handwriting as well as I know where all their moles are and what their voices sound like in a symphony of hundreds, so I was pretty sure that the letter hadn't been made by my son.

'Did you make this?' I asked, just to confirm my suspicions.

'No.'

'Who made this?'

'Mary – she's in my class.'

Now, some of the little girls in my son's class understand that I write for a magazine and that because of my job, my kids' pictures sometimes end up on the magazine's pages. As far as my boys' classmates are concerned, I'm enormously famous. They're also five and don't understand the difference between being Abu Dhabi-famous and being actually famous.

One girl, eager to see her face in print, asked me after school one afternoon if she could be in the magazine. When I needed generic shots a few weeks later, she was thrilled to pose. The girl is now pretty sure she's actually famous, which is fine by me.

In other words, it wouldn't be unreasonable for a girl in my son's class to write me a letter, only when I looked, I saw that the paper tucked inside the handmade envelope was quite clearly addressed to my oldest.

Though Mary had written one of the letters in my son's name backwards, there was no doubt the rainbows, smiley faces and purple hearts were directed at my boy with a passionate 'I loru you' at the end.

'Why are you giving me this?' I asked my oldest, interrupting a rousing debate he'd been having with his brother about which of them was more like Superman and which was more like Batman.

'It's nice. I fink you will like it.'

Apparently, even though Mary is a gorgeous little golden-haired, blue-eyed Swedish beauty who has already nearly mastered a second language, my son doesn't really like her 'that way'. But since it was obvious a lot of hard work had gone into her love letter, he thought it would be wasteful to simply throw it away so he re-gifted it to the girl of his actual dreams.

Which is still me.

I know I shouldn't be, but I'm pretty pleased about it. I wonder how Mary likes *them* apples.

* * *

And so, as I sit on the front porch drinking my coffee this morning watching the kids sail by on their new bikes, my youngest son four years and one day old, I realize that this is the dawn of the glory years.

My oldest is on the verge of reading and my youngest has almost completely mastered the toilet. He's even tall enough now to pee standing up rather than 'standing down'.

As of today, I've got two sweet, healthy little boys, a great relationship with a great guy and nobody has asked me if I'm pregnant in months. I'm in a pretty good mood most of the time, my job is going well and there's not much more I could ask for.

So what's it like having two kids? Well, you know how you felt when you realized that Cinderella was finally out of the clutches of her horrible stepfamily, or when Shrek kissed Fiona and she stayed an ogre, or when you clapped your hands and for no reason that could ever make sense Tinkerbell opened her eyes and flitted away, and you thought maybe everything was going to be alright after all?

Yeah, it's like that.

APPENDIX J: PEOPLE I APPRECIATE *A LOT*

- Dennis Jarrett, the editorial director of Abu Dhabi Week magazine, for hiring me, for letting me work flexible hours so that my children didn't go completely feral while I pursued my dream career, for believing in me and for giving me tons (sorry, *heaps*) of editorial feedback and encouragement, even if he did make me write in British English – I never would have *gotten* this far without you

- Samantha McBride for editorial support and for making me launch my writing career by assigning me my very first freelance job

- My dear friend Cindy Padgett for thinking I'm funny and laughing with me on our famous Gin and Tonic Play Dates – ewe are one hot little lamb chop

- Susan Van Hoogstraten and Stephanie Gauthier for loving my writing and for asking me 'When can I read it??' over and over until I finally finished it

- Anna Weaver, Barbara Fulton, Susie Thomas and Anna McCormack for all the feedback, comments and proofreading – you ladies are outstanding

- Scott Douglas and Richard Frost for designing and setting up my website in exchange for nothing more than brownies and beer – check out their great work and my blog at www.laurafulton.org

- Lucy and Russell for finding a home for my blind cat BeBe and her fat gay stepbrother Benji – 'Yule' always be special to me!

- My two little boys for making my life mean something and my beloved husband, for the dancing – and everything else

Made in the USA
Lexington, KY
13 May 2012